The

BREAD
and the
KNIFE

A LIFE IN 26 BITES

DAWN DRZAL

Arcade Publishing • New York

First Edition

Ferran Adrià's Liquid Pimento Olive recipe text appears courtesy of The Cooking Lab, LLC © The Cooking Lab, LLC

Christine's White Borscht recipe from *Soup Suppers* by Arthur Schwartz. Copyright © 1994 by Arthur Schwartz. Reprinted by permission of HarperCollins Publishers.

Every reasonable effort has been made to locate copyright holders and to obtain their permission for use of copyrighted material. The author and publisher would be grateful to be notified of any corrections that should be incorporated in future reprints or editions of this book.

Arcade Publishing books may be purchased in bulk at special discounts for sales promotion, corporate gifts, fund-raising, or educational purposes. Special editions can also be created to specifications. For details, contact the Special Sales Department, Arcade Publishing, 307 West 36th Street, 11th Floor, New York, NY 10018 or arcade@skyhorsepublishing.com.

Arcade Publishing® is a registered trademark of Skyhorse Publishing, Inc.®, a Delaware corporation.

Visit our website at www.arcadepub.com.
Visit the author's site at dawn-drzal.com.

10 9 8 7 6 5 4 3 2 1

Library of Congress Cataloging-in-Publication Data

Names: Drzal, Dawn, author.
Title: The bread and the knife : a life in 26 bites / Dawn Drzal.
Description: First edition. | New York : Arcade Publishing, [2018]
Identifiers: LCCN 2018012760 (print) | LCCN 2018014070 (ebook) | ISBN 9781628729245 (ebook) | ISBN 9781628729238 (alk. paper)
Subjects: LCSH: Drzal, Dawn. | Food writers—United States—Biography. | Cooking—Anecdotes.
Classification: LCC TX649.D79 (ebook) | LCC TX649.D79 A3 2018 (print) | DDC 641.5092 [B]—dc23
LC record available at https://lccn.loc.gov/2018012760

Cover design by Erin Seaward-Hiatt
Cover photo: iStockphoto

Printed in the United States of America

For Millie, who taught me to cook,
and
for John, who taught me everything else

When from a long distant past nothing subsists, after the people are dead, after the things are broken and scattered, still, alone, more fragile, but with more vitality, more unsubstantial, more persistent, more faithful, the smell and taste of things remain poised for a long time, like souls, ready to remind us, waiting and hoping for their moment, amid the ruins of all the rest; and bear unfaltering, in the almost impalpable drop of their essence, the vast structure of recollection.

—MARCEL PROUST, *REMEMBRANCE OF THINGS PAST*

You are the bread and the knife,
The crystal goblet and the wine.

—JACQUES CRICKILLON

CONTENTS

AUTHOR'S NOTE

For Imelda Marcos, it was shoes; for me, it's food. The organizing principle of my life. I don't mean to say that I live to eat, or that all I think about is food, although there have been times in my life when that was truer than it is now. I mean that food is the metaphor shaping how I view the world and what (or even whether) I remember. It's not as abstract as it sounds. The lunch of canned tomato soup and Saltines my first husband shared with me when we met—the shock of feeling suddenly at home with him over his cramped Formica table—is both a memory and a metaphor. Reader, that's why I married him. Perhaps this link explains my near-perfect recall when it comes to what I ate and relative amnesia about everything else. In any case, you can see why the gastronomical story of my life is the only one at my disposal.

"The events in our lives happen in a sequence in time," wrote Eudora Welty, "but in their significance to ourselves they find their own order." These chapters are organized alphabetically, but of course they occurred chronologically, so a timeline may be useful. I was born in

Philadelphia to ill-matched parents who divorced when I was five, and my mother remarried a questionable character six months later. Luckily, my maternal grandparents provided much-needed stability, and living with them between my mother's marriages, when I could pretend she was my feckless older sister, was the happiest period of my childhood. A few years after my stepfather entered the picture, my grandparents moved directly across the street from us. My mother was furious, but I suspect they knew I needed a normal family to balance out the drama at home. After college in New England, I moved to New York City, where I married the first man I met (he of the tomato soup and Saltines). Perhaps not surprisingly, we divorced ten years later. I became a book editor—cookbooks and science books mostly—and toward the end of my career I met my second husband. We had a son together and a good life, full of travel and wonderful meals, but that marriage ended after fifteen years. So here I am, still in New York, still on the lookout for the next good thing to eat. Life may disappoint, but gelato? Never.

The
BREAD
and the
KNIFE

is for

Al Dente

My grandmother was a genius in the kitchen, someone whose skill reliably transformed the simple into the sublime. One thing she could not master for the life of her, however, was timing. Dishes emerged from the kitchen at random while she flapped around the table like an enraged hen, shouting, *"Mangia! Mangia!* Eat it while it's hot!" and waving off our objections that we would be happy to wait or that she should sit down and join us.

Pasta accompanied many of these meals, so the nightly drama was regularly punctuated with the Testing of the Spaghetti. Even after fifty or sixty years, my grandmother claimed to be incapable of determining when pasta was al dente. At a certain point, standing over the roiling pot, she would call out in panicked voice, "Pop? Go find Pop!" No matter where my grandfather was, no matter which of his many hobbies he was pursuing—gardening, winemaking, listening to the ball game—he had to be fetched immediately. By the time he was located, minutes had usually passed, and the only way the spaghetti would have been al dente was if she had called him before she threw it into the boiling water. Nevertheless, she would heave a huge sigh of relief when he appeared, reprimand him for taking so long, and, after a few tries, succeed in capturing a few wily strands on a wooden spoon. These she would lift to his mouth (he was a foot taller than she was). "Perfect," he would say, after looking thoughtful for a moment, or sometimes, "It needs another minute." That couldn't possibly have been true, but you could tell it made her happy.

This charade, as I used to see it, drove me and everyone else in the family crazy. What was the point of bothering him? Why couldn't the woman test it herself, for God's sake, or use a timer, or let someone else do the tasting? It wasn't rocket science. My grandparents had been dead for many years before I understood that it wasn't about sense, or convenience. It was one of the rituals of love. My grandfather was central to the meal, it said. He was indispensable. His opinion was valued above all others. Despite how thin-skinned my grandmother was, she repeatedly braved our ridicule to tell him these things. When I left home and finally learned what al dente pasta tasted like, I realized she had sacrificed her perfectionism for sixty years to say in overcooked spaghetti what she could not put into words.

The rituals of love can take as many forms as love itself. They can be as elaborate as the Christmas Eve dinner that occupied my grandmother for the entire month of December or as humble as my stepfather's making me instant oatmeal every day for breakfast. God, I hated that oatmeal. I can still smell the fake maple flavoring and see the watery beige glop in the bowl. One morning when I was ten, I had a tantrum as soon as he left the kitchen, rattling the spoon around and around the bowl in a kind of frenzy while I talked out loud to myself. *How does he expect me to eat this slop? Who does he think he is? It's disgusting. This is fit for a pig!* Spooning up the oatmeal and slinging it back into the bowl, I felt someone staring at the back of my head. Filled with dread, I turned to see my stepfather standing in the kitchen doorway, wearing an expression of such naked hurt that the dread instantly turned to shame.

"I'm sorry," I stammered. "I didn't mean it."

But he had already begun walking down the hall to his room. He never made me breakfast again. I tried apologizing once more, but it was no use. It took me a long time to realize that he believed it was not the oatmeal but him I found wanting, and perhaps he was right. In any case, I learned that day that I had the fearsome power to wound another human being in a way that left a permanent scar.

After four years of drinking Carnation Instant Breakfast, I started high school at Nazareth Academy, which did not provide transportation for its students. My grandfather, who lived across the street, kindly offered to drive me to school every day on his way to work. Because, like most teenagers, I had trouble getting up on time, he also made me breakfast. He was as regular as clockwork. Never once in four years was he late, or sick, or short-tempered. I would come flying in the door ten minutes behind schedule, uniform half undone, and my coffee would be waiting with a saucer on top, still hot, with the milk and sugar already stirred in. I would object that I didn't have time to eat but would accept being overruled because, bratty as I still was, I had learned my lesson. Watching him stir the oatmeal in a saucepan (real oatmeal this time) or slice exactly half a banana onto my cornflakes with still-powerful but age-stiffened fingers, I knew that these were acts of love.

When my son was born, I knew only what not to do. The sole tools I had were the gifts my grandparents had given me: my grandmother's many expressions of love through cooking and my grandfather's daily example of absolute dependability. Our ritual had never varied, and the collective memory of those mornings buoyed me with a strength that was not my own, enabling me to get up with my son and make him breakfast every morning no matter how I felt, even during a dark year when I wished I were dying. Now, nearly grown, my son sits on a stool at the pass-through counter, eating an English muffin (no oatmeal for him) as we talk companionably about the upcoming day. Next week he will graduate from high school. It may sound ridiculous, but the fact that every day of his life has begun in exactly this gentle and consistent manner is a source of great pride for me. I have failed in many ways, but not this one.

There is something wonderfully redemptive about the idea—proposed in various forms by Native Americans, Aborigines, and Buddhists—that healing moves backward to our ancestors as well as forward to future generations. It makes a kind of sense. Having children forges a link with the past as well as the future: my ex-husband and I are related by blood through our son. Retroactively, whether we like it or not, we have become family. We are likewise irrevocably connected to each other's families, and so the bonds multiply through the generations. Why should it not be possible, then, for ancient hurts to be healed and future ones prevented through the faithful daily ritual of preparing breakfast?

is for

Béarnaise

When I told my stepfather I'd like to learn how to ski, he didn't choose a wholesome family resort in New England like Stowe or Sugarloaf for our winter vacation. Wholesome was a concept entirely foreign to him. He picked the Playboy Hotel at Great Gorge in nearby New Jersey, dubbed "the R-rated version of Disneyland" by *Skiing* magazine. Hardly the type of man who read *Skiing*, my stepfather probably heard about Great Gorge at the Playboy Club in Manhattan, where he paid twenty-five dollars a year for the privilege of being a "keyholder." From what I could tell, the only thing that key entitled him to was stealing hundreds of black-and-white bunny-head swizzle sticks, which turned up in various drawers for decades afterwards. Although the sprawling resort contained five restaurants, a nightclub, a three-level game room, an indoor swimming pool that converted to an enormous Jacuzzi, indoor tennis courts, and a health club, I spent most of my time on the Bunny slope, wiping out on the icy granules spewed by the snow machine. The only time I ever saw my parents was at meals, which would have suited me fine except for one thing: by December 1975, my sophomore year of high school, I had pretty much stopped eating.

Having lost more than twenty-five pounds since the previous summer, I weighed just 101 pounds at five feet five. Up until then, I had managed to disguise my growing emaciation beneath my Catholic school uniform. Designed to obscure the figure, the polyester pleated skirt, boxy buttoned "weskit," and blue blazer were what had gotten me into trouble in the first place. I simply hadn't noticed the pounds packing on until the summer before, when the girls with whom we shared our beach house started calling me "wide load" and I took a good look in the rearview mirror. It was true that I needed to lose a little weight, but at fifteen it was easy. I'd never known, until they pointed it out, that you could eat half an English muffin instead of a whole one, or that it wasn't a good idea to buy a half gallon of ice cream every Saturday night and eat it out of the carton with a spoon. It was an education.

The less I ate, the more I swam, rode my bike, and played tennis. As I watched the needle on the scale drop from 119 to 111 to 105, a dark elation took hold of me. Less was definitely more. I felt like a sculptor paring away everything that was unnecessary. Although a nagging voice told me it was time to stop, I didn't want to.

The psychic low point of that summer was my defeat by a small dish of vanilla ice cream at a decrepit soda fountain in Atlantic City. I had already lost fifteen pounds, and people had begun commenting on how good I looked. Part of me knew I deserved a treat. All day I had argued with myself about whether or not to order it, and by the time it arrived in a pedastaled stainless steel dish misted with cold and beaded with condensation, I was in such an agony of indecision that I rushed to the bathroom, sat on the toilet seat, and wept. When I came back to the table, I had made up my mind. The answer was, and would remain, "No." From then on, not a day passed during which I had eaten little enough to satisfy myself. I went to bed berating myself for what I had eaten that day and woke up plotting how little I could consume in the hours ahead. Like any obsession, it was exhausting, and part of me resented wasting so much valuable energy on something that felt so circular and, ultimately, unwinnable. By the time of the ski trip, five months later, my weight had reached a plateau from which it stubbornly refused to budge. No one talked about anorexia then, but I had a sense that to force my body further down would be to take a step from which there might be no turning back. I was still just sane enough to be afraid.

This vacation at Great Gorge was the first time in memory that my family had sat down together regularly for meals, and it didn't take long for my parents to notice that I ate practically nothing all day. At lunch on the second day, I must have come into focus for them for the first time in years. The meal is a blur except for the completely foreign experience of seeing fear in my mother's eyes, which quickly reverted to anger. She threatened to ground me when we got home until I gained five pounds—useless, since ordering me to put on weight was then tantamount to suggesting I set myself on fire. My stepfather, however, was too clever for a frontal attack. He made reservations three nights running at the VIP Room, the resort's "gourmet" restaurant. He knew I had loved fancy restaurants since I was a little girl. It had always delighted him that I ordered the most outré thing on the menu—frogs' legs or sweetbreads—although he himself rarely strayed from variations on prime rib.

The VIP Room may seem silly now, with its liveried "butlers" ceremoniously carving Chateaubriand for two, but the cooking was pure Escoffier. I would be lying if I went on to describe an exquisite meal, bite by bite. I most certainly did not sit down with the intention of enjoying myself—this was war. My memories of those three dinners are disoriented, conflated, strobe-lit. The decor, as befit the "Very Important Playboy," was all black, and the lighting so dim it was difficult to see the food. Flashbulbs of memory explode in the darkness: nearly fainting when I picked up the head of my filleted trout thinking it was a clam shell, my mother laughing, and a waiter whisking it away; the *whoosh* of Steak Diane igniting tableside; a bite of shrimp with a yellow sauce. And here the lights go on. The yellow sauce was without doubt the most delicious thing I had ever put in my mouth. Buttery, tangy, tinged with some vaguely licorice-y herb. I forgot to be self-conscious and asked the waiter what the sauce was, what the herb was (Béarnaise, tarragon). I also forgot, for the first time in months, that I wasn't supposed to be eating. When the guilt returned, which it did with a wallop to my gut, a huge protest welled up inside me. For a moment, I had stepped off the seesaw of yes and no onto *terra incognita*, and I did not want to climb back on. Those few bites had had nothing to do with whether I denied myself or allowed myself to indulge in a known quantity like vanilla ice cream. They had represented the excitement of the unknown, the taste of the world I knew was out there and couldn't wait to escape to. The hunger in me to experience that was stronger, if just barely, than the voice that said no. While I was still teetering on the great gorge—you can't make these things up—this meal lured me back from the edge. Always a shrewd judge of character, my stepfather was absolutely right to sidestep the issue of power—my parents' over me, mine over myself—and appeal to my sense of adventure.

Recently, through a combination of luck and some truly obsessive digging on the Internet, I managed to track down the *chef de saucier* of the VIP Room from 1975. Not much older than I was at that time, he now teaches at the Cornell Hotel School. He could not explain to me how the Béarnaise sauce, which was served with beef, found its way onto my shrimp. It is possible that I mentally combined the shrimp from one meal with the sauce from another, but the sauce I remember perfectly. Here is the chef's recollection of the version I ate that night:

> *As I remember the Béarnaise sauce for the Chateaubriand and the filet mignon was a reduction of fresh tarragon, tarragon vinegar, and a very dry white wine. It was reduced by one-half and brought to room temperature (this is important to not break the end sauce). We then clarified whole butter and cracked and separated egg yolks into a very clean mixing bowl. Using a bain-marie, we would then slowly whip the yolks over a moist heat until they start to thicken. Be careful not to overheat the eggs as you will have scrambled eggs*

instead. Once the egg mixture becomes rather thick, we start to slowly incorporate the butter into the egg mixture. Once the fluffiness is achieved, we then slowly incorporate some of the tarragon mixture to taste (please not too strong and maintain a thicker-than-nappe consistency). The goal is to achieve light and fluffy with a prevalent tarragon flavor. At the very end, a squeeze of lemon to brighten the dense flavor of the yolk. You can finish with chiffonade of fresh basil or tarragon. I prefer to leave the sauce like the sun, bright and yellow. I hope this brings a wonderful memory back to life.

Beginning to question whether a mere sauce could have saved me from borderline anorexia, I came across a quote from Baron Brisse, sometimes referred to as the world's first food journalist. A man of enormous girth, who had to pay double to get on the nineteenth-century equivalent of a bus, he wrote of Sauce Béarnaise, "It frightens me! With it, one might never stop eating." Clearly, I had august company in believing that Béarnaise was more than a sauce; it was a force.

Twenty years later, I was sitting at a large round table at French Laundry, Thomas Keller's legendary restaurant in Yountville, California. The Sauce Béarnaise had done its job so effectively that I had become a cookbook editor, and the chef had designed a tasting menu for six of us to showcase the proposal for his first cookbook, which I was considering. Across the table sat my husband's new business partner and his girlfriend, whom I had met for the first time earlier that day, horribly hungover by the pool. After running to the bathroom several times, she claimed she had eaten something that hadn't agreed with her the night before. My husband had told me she was a single mother and knew she wasn't getting any younger. She desperately wanted the man to marry her, and it was vital that she look good in a bikini. Claiming not to be an adventurous eater, she accepted a sourdough roll but declined every one of the fifty-three astonishing dishes that came out of the kitchen. At some point, I realized it was useless to urge her to taste the eggcup of White Truffle Oil–Infused Custard with Black Truffle Ragout or even the Salad of Petite Summer Tomatoes with Vine-Ripe Tomato Sorbet in the hope that she might find her own "Sauce Béarnaise." It had been too many years since she sacrificed her body to the jealous gods of anorexia and alcohol. So she sat alone in the middle of the feast, rolling her bread into little white pills that she washed down one by one with a swallow of red wine.

is for

Crab

"Dawn! What have you done for me lately?" The booming voice on the other end of the line was unmistakable even though I hadn't heard it for six or seven years: it was the famous David Halberstam rumble, a basso profundo you could feel in your molars. From anyone else, the question might have been a joke, although not in the best of taste as the first thing to say after such a long time. But from Halberstam, it was a literal question. If I had not done anything to benefit him in the years since we had seen each other, then as far as he was concerned, those years were wasted. Needless to say, our conversation was brief.

I lost my editorial virginity to Halberstam when I was twenty-four. Called in as reinforcement for the flagging Tom Congdon, whose mental and physical health were being ruined by the task of trying to tame the massive manuscript that was to become *The Reckoning*, I was sent home by the publisher with a desktop computer (it was the mid-eighties) and instructions not to come back until it had been cut by three hundred pages. In the battle of life, Tom was no match for David: Halberstam was a predator—wiry and hawk-like, his nose straining to meet his chin—while the genteel and diffident Tom, whose smooth face and enormous forehead recalled an overgrown baby, was prey. Whatever else you could say about Halberstam, you could never accuse him of laziness—he always needed two editors, even at the *New York Times*. But if his output was prodigious, it was also undigested. When I sat down at the scroll-legged mahogany library table that served as my desk, the first sentence I read was, "Henry Ford was a charismatic man of charisma." And so it continued. No wonder Tom had actually had an epileptic seizure, possibly induced, his doctor said, by thousands of hours spent staring at a flickering computer screen.

Any notion I'd entertained that staying home to edit was going to be a vacation was quickly squelched. I worked twelve hours a day, six days a week, and Halberstam's mountainous manuscript blanketed every surface of the living room from February to May. Years later, a boyfriend who also worked in the business asked me, "Why is it that every time you have to edit a manuscript, it's like you're scaling Everest?" My answer was, "Because I am." Only in the case of *The Reckoning*, however, was it physically true. Eventually, the manuscript was safely turned over to the production department. Tom's health improved, and as a gesture of thanks he gave me a first edition of M. F. K. Fisher's *The Gastronomical Me* and took me to dinner at La Colombe d'Or.

Perhaps for Tom it was just one of many enjoyable meals that studded his publishing career, but that dinner marked the beginning of my gastronomic and professional coming of age. La Colombe d'Or was a little piece of Provence tucked in an old brownstone on East 26th Street. Stepping beneath the pretty striped awning past the flower boxes full of geraniums and ivy that screened the subterranean entrance from the street, I felt we had just exited the Train Bleu rather than the Lexington Avenue subway. We were led past curtained windows flung open to the late spring breeze to a banquette covered with blue Provençal fabric. Tom ordered two glasses of champagne as an aperitif—so soigné, I thought, surprised that one could order glasses without ordering a bottle and filing the information away where I would call upon it for the next twenty-five years, until I stopped drinking entirely. We perused the brief menu, penned in spiky French script. It was composed of seasonal and regional dishes, unusual in an era when French still meant either stuffy old-school classic or *nouvelle cuisine*. One of the entrees was soft-shell crabs, which Tom was politely surprised to hear I had never eaten before and insisted I order. I don't recall the first course; I only remember the shock of that first bite of soft-shell crab *meunière*, citric sharpness mellowed by toasty brown butter, the peculiar resistance of the shell, the squirt of saline succeeded by something squishy and undifferentiated that didn't bear thinking about, and then the awful moment when I wondered if I would be able to chew and swallow what felt like a mouthful of shrimp shells. Happily, I forced myself. Taken together, the combination of sensations was thrilling, like some sort of initiation. I couldn't wait to take another bite.

Dessert was another first that Tom was delighted to introduce me to: *fraises des bois*, wild strawberries, which— I learned that night—have nothing in common with grocery store strawberries but the name. A bowl of irregular rubies, each shading to translucent scarlet at the edge, served unadorned (how apt of the French to say *nature* to mean "plain"). Perhaps there was some *crème fraiche* or *crème anglaise* on the side, but I remember only the incredible concentration of taste and color, the intensity and miniature perfection of those simple berries. Sitting on the banquette as Tom safely flirted with me from his married, middle-aged vantage, I felt a vague aspiration forming. I could not have articulated it, but the evening had lifted a curtain on a civilized approach to the world, almost a philosophy, in which the pleasure of being an adult lay in the intelligent satisfaction of the appetites. Although I eventually discovered that I lacked the discipline for that sort of restrained hedonism, soft-shell crabs have never lost their fascination for me. They are the food of liminality, of that magical period of unlimited potential when one identity has been shed and the next has not yet been assumed.

is for

Dinner Party

By a rough estimate, I threw about a hundred dinner parties over the course of my first decade in New York. During my twenties and early thirties, few things gave me more pleasure than inviting six or seven people over to eat a complicated dish I had read about and researched, a much more time-consuming and serendipitous process in the years before every recipe imaginable was instantly accessible on the Internet. My favorite dishes were elaborate peasant productions that people had spent generations arguing about: choucroute garnie and paella, bourride and tagine. No doubt it was the only child in me trying to reproduce the holiday atmosphere of extended family gatherings, when the dinner table would suddenly swell from its usual two or three to twelve and beyond. My policy of never making any recipe twice kept life exciting, but it resulted in the occasional spectacular failure like one evening's chicken in a bulletproof salt crust. When the hammer and screwdriver suggested by the recipe proved useless, I tried dropping it on the kitchen floor, where it chipped a terra-cotta tile and rolled behind the refrigerator like a lumpy basketball. When the armor finally yielded to a crowbar retrieved from the trunk of a neighbor's car, it was revealed that instead of roasting to golden brown perfection, the bird had steamed into something resembling a shrunken head.

Nevertheless, most of these dinners were pleasant, and many were delightful. Just one, however, stands out in my memory as perfect. It took place on December 27, 1990—a date I can verify because, at some point during the evening, an unexpected snowstorm began blanketing the city. The day before, my husband and I had flown back from a Christmas visit to my parents, who had loaded our carry-on bags with an enormous uncooked *porchetta*, two bottles of excellent Margaux, one of green Chartreuse, and two boxes of liqueur-filled chocolates. One of the advantages of being relatively young and poor was that we could share our eclectic windfall without the fear of being judged. It was the twenty-something version of sharing a care package at camp. Like much of our hospitality then, it had an impromptu purity that I never managed to recapture in later, flusher years.

Reaching about five answering machines, we realized that the usual suspects were out of town for the holidays. Forced to put some actual thought into the guest list, I reread the last chapter of M. F. K. Fisher's *An Alphabet for Gourmets*, in which she states that gastronomical perfection can be reached in a dinner for six people: "two beautiful, one intelligent, three of correlated professions such as architecture, music, and photography." She then elaborates, "A good combination would be one married couple . . . one less firmly established . . . and two strangers of either sex, upon whom the better-acquainted diners could sharpen their questioning wits." Upon reading those words, it struck me that my previous guest lists had suffered from a fundamental error: I had approached them like menus composed of a series of loosely related dishes when I should have viewed them as recipes, taking into account the complex chemical reactions between the guests. I deviated from the rest of her advice only in the number of invitees. It seemed like a waste to cook for six people when you could have eight.

My husband and I had recently moved into a floor-through brownstone apartment in Carroll Gardens. Brooklyn then was still considered ultima Thule by

Manhattanites, cut off from the mainland, and Carroll Gardens was best known as the neighborhood where Italian mobsters housed their elderly parents. But the apartment was lovely: during the day its high-ceilinged, well-proportioned rooms were flooded with light from triple windows at the front and back. With the arrival of evening, the dim central room turned into a cave illuminated by candlelight. On that evening, we had arrayed in the living room our usual assortment of baba ghanoush, taramosalata, and luscious purple Kalamata olives from Sahadi's, the Lebanese food emporium on Atlantic Avenue. Alongside were piles of *laham ajeen*—a sort of Middle Eastern pizza—and za'atar bread from the neighboring Damascus Bakery. The first guests to arrive were my closest friend and her husband, fellow Brooklynites who lived in neighboring Park Slope. Married since graduate school, they filled M. F. K. Fisher's "married couple" category. By contrast, my husband and I, married a little over a year, were in the "less firmly established" camp. Even before they took off their coats, they were drawn into the kitchen by the aroma of roasting pork stuffed with crushed garlic, fennel seeds, hot pepper, and herbs, which seemed atavistically designed to get the ghrelin flowing. The buzzer began ringing again, admitting the rest of the guests in ones and twos. Each guest knew at least two other people, but I was the only person to know everyone, so there was both sufficient comfort and plenty of opportunity for wit-sharpening. The smell of the *porchetta* incited everyone to consume vast quantities of hors d'oeuvres washed down with copious amounts of Penfold's Koonunga Hill, the house wine at that time. Their needs taken care of for the moment, I was free to observe that my guests certainly fulfilled Fisher's requirements. All were intelligent (one was brilliant), two were beautiful, and six of the eight were in correlated professions: book and magazine publishing, writing, teaching (literature), and theater criticism (the other two were lawyers, but one of them was my husband and the other was so handsome he could be forgiven almost anything). Fisher's formula, if it doesn't sound cold to call it that, was working like a charm. My best friend's husband—a magazine editor and fiction writer—was peppering the large-chinned, handsome litigator about arcane points of courtroom procedure for a noir novel he was writing. The assistant editor, a long-legged ingénue endearingly unaware of her beauty and bemused about why she was there with the grownups, gamely discussed feminist theory with my novelist best friend before they settled into a wicked exchange of gossip about a mutual acquaintance. My husband was in his element—intellectual conversation. I could see the ghosts of his parents sitting in approval at either elbow as he first weighed in on the feminist theory discussion before moving on to take issue with the theater critic about her recent pan of a Caryl Churchill play. I asked the brilliant literature professor, whose true love was theology, what he thought of the idea of my commissioning a biography of Hildegard von Bingen that would include a CD of her music and somehow ended up hearing his thoughts about Thomas Aquinas and the Trinity. Within moments, interactions among the guests began forming and dissolving like complex molecules in a volatile solution, some bonds stronger, some weaker, so that conversations of two merged into four and six and then separated and reconfigured into odd numbered groupings. Soon I was too caught up to admire it.

The hors d'oeuvres had long been decimated when the *porchetta* was finally ready. As we stood to filter into the dining room, everyone drained his wineglass in preparation for the Margaux aerating on the sideboard. In the center of the dining room, my grandmother's fruitwood dining table glowed like a candlelit island. We had dispensed, as usual, with a first course, and thick slices of *porchetta* were fanned out on a platter in the center of the table. Beside it was a huge bowl of Potatoes Fontecchio, a recipe from *The Silver Palate Good Times Cookbook*. They were delicious enough to be one of the sole exceptions to my rule of never repeating a dish: whole new potatoes roasted until nearly dessicated, cut in half and tossed while still hot with loads of minced garlic, extra-virgin olive oil, fresh mint, salt, and pepper. Flanking the candlesticks were a basket of fresh semolina bread with sesame seeds from the Italian bakery on Court Street and a watercress and endive salad.

When all the plates and glasses were filled, I paused to enjoy the lull of hungry people eating, the clinking of flatware punctuated only by appreciative murmuring. And then there arrived the moment I had been waiting for without realizing I was waiting for it, the real—if unacknowledged—reason I gave dinner parties in the first place: the moment when time stood still and I was suddenly suffused with the unassailable certainty that all was right with the world, a sense of sublime connection not only with my guests but also with whatever it is that makes eating the bread and drinking the cup the ultimate metaphor of spiritual communion. These moments were my secret, the closest thing I had to a religion. Until I read the dinner party scene in Virginia Woolf's *To the Lighthouse* a few years later, in one of those exceedingly rare encounters in literature when we come across something so private that we have barely attempted to articulate it even to ourselves, I thought I was the only person to feel precisely this sensation. It was a shock to recognize myself in Mrs. Ramsay's joy as she served the boeuf en daube ("a perfect triumph") to her guests: "It partook, she felt, carefully helping Mr. Bankes to a specially tender piece, of eternity. . . . Of such moments, she thought, the thing is made that endures." This feeling unconsciously emanating from the guests, that we constituted an island against the darkness outside, made all the trouble of shopping and cooking and cleanup worthwhile. It was grace, produced by what Fisher calls "the alchemy of hospitality."

What distinguished my perfect dinner party from all the others was that the moment didn't evaporate at the beginning of the meal; it dilated, surviving even the transition back to the brightness of the living room. Without interrupting the single kaleidoscopic conversation that had begun over hors d'oeuvres hours earlier, our guests rearranged themselves on the sofa, the armchair, the ottoman, the floor, sipping Chartreuse and making occasional forays into the boxes of foil-wrapped chocolate bottles filled with liqueurs that sat on the coffee table. There was something endearingly silly about the facsimile wrappings and the peculiar, crunchy lining of alcohol-soaked sugar. My hostess duties discharged, I sat tucked into the corner of the ivory chenille sofa nearest the stereo where my husband was happily playing DJ with his prized record collection.

At some point later, all conversation abruptly stopped— one of those unaccountable "angel passing over" silences, as if an invisible hand had been held up. And then we heard it, or rather we didn't: an eerie, neutron bomb, middle of the country stillness, wrong for Brooklyn. Running to the window, the ingénue raised the blinds to reveal an opaque curtain of pure white. Huge, heavy, steady flakes had blurred the familiar outlines of the street, like a white duvet thrown hastily over bunched-up bed-clothes. Someone looked at his watch and exclaimed disbelievingly that it was four o'clock in the morning. How had we all lost track of so many hours? It was the snow that, in muffling the street noises, had silenced the subconscious chronometer that city dwellers use to keep track of time.

Suddenly, everyone was up, putting on coats, saying their goodbyes. A plan was hatched that the Manhattan contingent would walk across the Brooklyn Bridge and the Park Slope contingent set off for home through Boerum Hill. My husband and I, glad not to have to brave the cold, stuck our heads out the window, arms around each other's waists, to watch them whooping and laughing through the unmarked whiteness, until they split into two groups at the corner and went their separate ways.

About fifteen years after that evening, I was staying at the Inn at Shelburne Farms in Vermont with my second hus-band and our young son. Glancing up from my book on the lawn one afternoon, I saw the ingénue for the first time in a decade, sitting under a tree a stone's throw away. She was so deep in conversation with another young woman that their foreheads were almost touching. If I had thought about it, I wouldn't have interrupted, but she was so completely unchanged that the intervening years seemed to disappear, and I found myself standing in front of her and saying hello. She was polite enough to try to suppress a visible wave of irritation at being intruded upon, but when she looked at my face, it was as if she were surfacing from a great depth. After I repeated my name, she remembered who I was, but the warmth I expected didn't accompany the recognition. Without introducing me to her friend, she told me she was getting married at the inn that weekend. I congratulated her and she thanked me, but she regarded me so coldly that I realized it was intended as a dismissal. I was clearly a petty irritation, like a fly that had landed on her dinner. Flushing, I hurriedly said goodbye and retrieved my book with as much dignity as I could muster.

Walking up the steps to my room, I lifted my palm to my burning cheek. I understood from experience how she could have replaced her former life so thoroughly with a new one. But the shock of seeing that I had ended up on her memory's cutting-room floor clarified that, until that moment, I had harbored the strange delusion that my old experiences were preserved somewhere, like a childhood bedroom. That they were still enacted, in some shadowy form, by the ghosts of the people who had shared them with me. Years earlier, in a periodic replaying of the dinner party in my mind, I realized that my relationship with every last person there—even the bond that was supposed to last forever—had turned out to be as ephemeral as the meal. This woman had been a player in the drama, and here she was in the flesh having forgotten all about it (about me!). That meant that my treasured memory was not a talisman I shared with all the others, not a mystical continuity transcending our ruptured connections, but merely a re-creation I had staged in my mind and obsessively revisited. As I looked out at the whitecaps of Lake Champlain, I forced myself to summon up how each of those relationships had ended. It amounted to a catalog of human frailties, mostly mine. But as the bird said in T. S. Eliot's *Four Quartets*, "human kind / Cannot bear very much reality." So I sank onto the faded chaise longue and ran the dinner party again from the top, putting the ingénue through her paces one more time—running to the window, whooping through the snow. Back where she belonged.

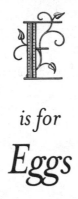

is for

Eggs

When I was a senior in high school, my mother kindly (and, I see in retrospect, wisely) offered to prepare a buffet so I could bring a bunch of friends home after the December prom. Despite expensive efforts at remodeling, our cavernous finished basement remained intractably dank, a room visited regularly only to empty the bucket of the dehumidifier. No one was going to watch TV on an icy black Naugahyde sofa in a basement whose chill penetrated the soles of your shoes even through the carpeting. The other furniture intensified the room's gloomy air: in one distant corner a massive carved "Spanish-style" bar and in the other a table and chairs constructed from whisky barrels and more black Naugahyde. Still, it was private, and more comfortable than the backseat of a car.

Only one thing can distract a teenage male from large platters of hot food, and I recall a puppyish stampede down the stairs past a table laden with enough fare for a small wedding reception. Hours later, hunger prompted some of the boys to lead their dates over to check out the row of rectangular chafing dishes whose Sterno had long since burned out. Under the lids were baked ziti, lasagna, beef Stroganoff with egg noodles—carefully prepared, now cold and congealed. Nevertheless, the trays were soon cleaned out with locust-like efficiency, and the couples melted back into the gloom. All that remained were some scrambled eggs whose liquid had separated in a milky pool at one end of the serving dish. My stomach felt imperiously empty, so I reluctantly took a few spoonfuls. To my astonishment, they were delicious. They tasted like my grandmother's eggs. The next morning, I congratulated my mother. "You finally did it! You made eggs as good as Grandmom's. They were even amazing cold." She smiled and shook her head. "They were Grandmom's eggs. She came over to help me last night after you left." Genius will out.

There is a reason why chefs ask prospective employees to make an omelette. It is in this, the simplest of dishes, that the cook's hand is laid bare. There is nowhere to hide in an omelette, and the touch of genius, if there is any, will be revealed. My maternal grandmother had the touch. Whatever she made—whether it was one of the scores of traditional Italian dishes she knew by heart or something complicated from a cookbook or food magazine—was at least delicious and often exquisite. Not surprisingly, her gift was most apparent in her eggs. She didn't even make omelettes—she did homeliness one better and made scrambled eggs. As absurd as it may sound, they were, without exception (and I ate them hundreds of times), sublime. They had an elusive quality of pure dairy sweetness that I have never encountered elsewhere, in any home kitchen or restaurant, and that I have been attempting without success to replicate all my life. Once or twice I have captured a hint of it, I never figured out by what accident, and years passed between successes. She used no secret ingredient, no special pan, no arcane technique, because I watched her like a hawk for two decades from the breaking of the eggs (regular white supermarket eggs, taken straight from the refrigerator) to the serving plate. It was maddening. Everything was too simple, too flexible. She used anywhere from one to ten eggs, although two to six seemed to work best. After breaking them into a bowl—she preferred shallow to deep, I noticed, and glass to metal or plastic—she would add either a splash of milk or a bit of cold water from the tap and a pinch of salt (usually plain old iodized Morton's). Then she would beat the eggs with a fork—and this may be where the magic came in. There was a special sound to her beating, a subdued *glop*. She was gentle with the eggs, but not too gentle. (Do I remember her saying, *Be nice to your eggs and they'll be nice to you*, or did I make that up?) She was just forceful enough that under her fork they turned a beautiful pale lemon yellow; generating very few bubbles, she beat just until they were completely emulsified, not a second longer. Meanwhile, a pat of butter would be melting in a pan (small ancient Teflon or large cast iron, depending on quantity) over medium low heat. It didn't even matter what kind of butter she used, but the one cardinal rule was that the eggs should *never* brown. She gently moved the cooked part aside with a spatula so that the runny part moved into the empty bottom of the pan and cooked them just until they were set, no longer glossy but not quite matte. Part of their deliciousness lay in their shape: in the last moment, they formed themselves into large, organic curds that needed to be served whole, so that cutting into them was like cutting into a steaming quenelle.

The memory of their texture and color lingers, and I can almost smell them still, but as the years pass that indefinable sweetness is like a beloved person's voice that I can no longer hear in my mind's ear. I recapture a scintilla of it only on the rare occasions when I succeed in producing it myself. In my quest, I have experimented with milk versus water, fork versus whisk, shallow bowl versus deep, different pans, different heat, and most of all different beating techniques. I take a few deep breaths, try to channel my grandmother, to hear the rhythm of the fork against the bowl, to reproduce the *glop*, to minimize the bubbles, to recreate that pale lemon yellow. But what sets a great cook apart from a merely good one—the culinary Midas touch that makes the humblest thing she prepares taste ineffably, irreproducibly delicious—will always be a mystery.

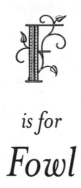

is for

Fowl

Before I was old enough to know that you should never meet your heroes, I dreamed of writing a biography of M. F. K. Fisher. An editor I knew wrote me a letter of introduction, and for several years I flew out to California to interview her when I could afford it and pored over her papers in Radcliffe's Schlesinger Library the rest of the time.

On one of these visits, her caregiver-*cum*-companion left soon after I arrived, dressed as the Statue of Liberty. She announced she would be gone all day for the Golden Gate Bridge Celebration. After enlisting my help with a few surreptitious tasks of which that lady would not approve, Fisher turned her wheelchair to face me and asked, "Do you like pheasant, dear?" Of course, I said I loved it. She could have asked me if I liked excrement and the answer would have been the same. She pointed to the kitchen. "There's a nice fresh pheasant on the counter. An orphan boy shot it for me this morning." An orphan boy? She looked me over appraisingly. "You can cook dinner for me, dear. You'd like that, wouldn't you." It was a statement rather than a question. My heart began pounding crazily. It was like being asked to play the violin for Paganini without having a chance to practice.

While she went to rest, I examined the pheasant, which had a couple of lead slugs embedded in one of its hugely muscled thighs. They were the thighs of an Olympic sprinter. Nice and fresh indeed. Weren't pheasants supposed to be hung? I had known Mary Frances long enough to begin to suspect that this was some bizarre test, not only of my cooking skills but also of my mettle, as if writing her biography were a secret society and this was part of the hazing ritual. Then I got a brilliant idea: braising with sauerkraut! The combination of the technique and the enzymes would tenderize even this monster. When she got up, I shared my idea with her. I saw a spark of respect kindle in her eye. "I always keep a few cans of sauerkraut in the cupboard, dear. You won't even have to go out shopping." And then she told me she always rinsed her sauerkraut, to prevent it from being too salty. This went against my instincts, especially since I was counting on the brine to tenderize the meat, but who was I to argue with Paganini?

The pheasant looked very respectable, browned and nestled between layers of sauerkraut studded with juniper berries in one of her ancient Dutch ovens. It might not be the pheasant *sous cloche* she had ordered on the train to Chicago with her uncle, commemorated so gloriously in *The Gastronomical Me*, but with any luck it would be edible. As I put the lid on the pot and slid it into the oven, I said a silent prayer. Two hours later, the kitchen was redolent with a promising smell and Mary Frances pronounced that she was hungry. I had set the round table with wine glasses and her green Mexican plates, put out a bowl of buttery red new potatoes and a salad made from gorgeous lettuces left as offerings by various admirers. Although crippled with arthritis and Parkinson's, Mary Frances did not believe in eating in her wheelchair. With great effort, leaning heavily on her cane, she transferred herself into a dining chair. Lifting the cover released a billow of tangy, meaty steam. I breathed a sigh of relief. "Would you like a nice slice of breast?" I asked, praying she would say yes to the part that was likely to be the tenderest because I could slice it paper thin. But she never gave the easy answer. "Oh no, dear," she said. "I'd like a leg." I sighed, knowing better than to resist. There was nothing to do but serve it to her. First, she tasted the sauerkraut, making a little moue of displeasure. "This has no taste, dear. Sauerkraut is supposed to be sour." I could feel spots of pink spring to my cheeks. The injustice of it! I would never have washed it if she hadn't told me to! But before I could decide whether to respond, she picked up the leg with both hands and took an enormous bite from the thigh. I looked down, awaiting the verdict. Nothing. I looked at her apprehensively. Could it take that long to chew? It must be even tougher than I had feared. And then I realized, to my horror, that she had not said anything because she could not speak—that bite of pheasant was lodged in her throat. She was turning crimson, her eyes very wide. I stood up. "Are you all right?" I asked inanely. "Can I help you? Is there someone I can call? A doctor?" I rushed over to the phone, but there were no emergency numbers there. Her face was now almost purple. I began to get really worried, the kind where you get very calm. "Do you want me to do the Heimlich maneuver on you?" A look of supreme annoyance crossed her face, superseding the fear for a moment. She flapped her hands, waving me away. I thought of clapping her between the shoulder blades, but she was so birdlike I was afraid I'd break her vertebrae. A headline flashed before my eyes in black-and-white newsprint: ASPIRING BIOGRAPHER KILLS M. F. K. FISHER.

BELOVED AUTHOR DEAD AT 80. I resolved to do the Heimlich even if it meant hurting her, but just as I walked behind her, she gave a massive cough and a piece of meat flew out of her mouth and across the room. "Oh, my God," I stammered, "I am so sorry. I tried, I mean I knew it would be tough . . . I wanted you to have the breast." She stopped me cold with a look. Her color was returning to normal. She took a gulp of wine. "I'll stick to this," she said. "It's safer."

I nattered away for the next few minutes, trying to make things feel normal again. She was so drained by her ordeal that she seemed hardly aware of my presence, but I still kept talking. Although she hadn't appeared to move, her wineglass suddenly shattered with splintering force on the black tile floor. I sprang up, my skirt soaked, wet shards around my feet. She looked at me, her blue eyes suddenly very focused. "You'd better get a broom," she said. And then, "I'll bet you think I did that on purpose, don't you, dear?"

is for

Gruel

One of my favorite picture books is *The Doubtful Guest* by Edward Gorey, a delightfully macabre little tale of a peculiar creature who appears one night on the doorstep of an overbred Edwardian family. Once he darts inside, there is no getting rid of him, and seventeen years later he is still eating the plates and hiding all the towels. Houseguests being what they are, one needn't look far for Gorey's inspiration. My own "doubtful guest" was my second husband's college roommate, who seemed to come along for the ride when we moved in together. Although he didn't stay continuously for the fourteen years he made himself at home in our apartment, he took up residence three or four times a year for about a month at a time. Given the spatial restrictions of Manhattan real estate, this was a problem, especially since he slept in my study and his habit of rising late was exacerbated by a resolute adherence to Pacific Standard Time. A light sleeper, he was so unpleasant when awakened before three p.m. that we all tiptoed around until he got up, whereupon he invariably claimed not to have slept a wink.

Arguably worse than his usurpation of my study for a month at a time was his commandeering of the kitchen. I should state for the record that I am not someone who can't stand people in "my" kitchen. I wouldn't even have minded particularly if he ate what was in the larder, although the one time in all those years that I asked him to pick up something at the store, he left me the receipt with $1.49 circled, so that I could reimburse him for the bananas. The problem was one of occupation. Once he took over the stove, he was there to stay—on and off—for the next three or four hours, despite the fact that I needed to prepare dinner for my family. It seemed doubly unfair that he should be in my study when I wanted to work and in the kitchen when I wanted to cook, yet like the over-polite Edwardians in *The Doubtful Guest*, I seemed unable to confront him when my oblique suggestions were neatly deflected.

I would have been happy to cook for Aloysius (that really should have been his name), but he inhabited an alternate culinary universe. Actually, culinary is the wrong word; it implies that what he consumed was food. He is the one person I've met who would have lost nothing by being fed through a tube. His day invariably began (nine hours after ours did) with the concoction of a complicated gruel prepared according to a strict rotation schedule. Monday might be amaranth day (which my son hated because of the lingering smell), Tuesday buckwheat, Wednesday millet, and so on. These grains, carefully measured out of dusty plastic bags from the bulk bin, were boiled for thirty to forty minutes while being stirred with a wooden paddle. When the contents had been transferred to a bowl, the scorched pot was half filled with water, the coagulated paddle left afloat, where they would remain until someone in the household became sufficiently disgusted to wash them. Assorted seeds, oils, and powders were then stirred into the mush. When it was finished, it looked and smelled like boiled newspaper. Providing Aloysius with roughly half of his daily caloric intake, his breakfast Oobleck concluded with a dessert of exactly seven berries. He was very insistent that one needed to consume only seven berries to enjoy their full nutritional benefit. It should come as no surprise that a man of average height who thinks seven blueberries constitutes a serving should weigh 120 pounds. The serving size question, about which he felt an almost religious fervor, gave a clue to the modus operandi behind his eating habits: controlled undereating masquerading as an obsession with health. I don't presume to understand his psychic makeup, but Aloysius had made an art form of living on $9,000 a year since college, and you can't do that if you eat as much as a normal person. Although he claimed to be writing a screenplay for most of the time he lived with us, the hours not devoted to preparing food seemed to be spent on the phone bullying and wheedling hapless customer service representatives into giving him things for free. Living on practically nothing is a full-time job. In one particular area, though, his obsessive thrift clearly belied his obsession with health: he would routinely consume foodstuffs long after their expiration date, appearance, and/or smell indicated they should have been tossed.

His second daily foray into the kitchen occurred about an hour after gruel consumption: time to bake his daily quick bread. Baking posed a challenge not only because of the strict grain rotation schedule but also because Aloysius was allergic to yeast and sugar. He often related with grim relish the story of how he had felt his throat closing up the last time he'd had a milkshake (thirty years earlier), and he was certain he would go into anaphylactic shock if he put any sugar in his system. When our small son pressed a few pieces of candy corn into his hand one Halloween, Aloysius stared at his palm as if it held pellets of rat poison. "Wow," he said, on his way to the bathroom to wash his hands. "Thanks. How about if I just smell it later?" Not that his hypochondria was a secret. He had a Proustian horror of drafts and, like Gorey's Doubtful Guest, was rarely without a woolen muffler. The first time I met him, at a restaurant in June, I was surprised to see him swathed to the ears, but my fiancé just laughed indulgently and told me that Aloysius viewed air-conditioning as his personal nemesis. Despite the fact that no diva could have protected her throat more assiduously, he was always "coming down" with something, and his nasal ablutions were a frequent topic of conversation.

An hour or so after the bread came out of the oven, it was time to prepare the evening "meal," a plain steamed vegetable with either brown rice pasta or barely seasoned protein (tofu, fish) topped with crumbled quick bread for bulk. This hodgepodge was sometimes packed in a Tupperware container, to be consumed in furtive bites outside whatever theater he happened to have gotten discount tickets to, punctuated with sips from the plastic water bottle he filled from our Poland Spring dispenser.

Since he was also allergic to anything fermented (soy sauce, vinegar, alcohol) and many miscellaneous foods that I now mercifully forget, it was impossible to include him in household meals. I kept a list of the offenders on the side of the refrigerator, but even when I was triumphantly convinced I'd avoided all minefields in that night's family dinner, he'd look at me with a sad little smile and say something like, "Sorry, today is not a corn day."

Finally, after fourteen years, we offered him an ultimatum: a deadline to move out of my study in exchange for the exclusive occupancy of the maid's room. He turned us down. Although he didn't come right out and say so, he was clearly holding out for the study, which was larger. When he finally left and we had unrestricted access to our own apartment again, it was hard to believe we had tolerated his presence for so long. It felt like being suddenly cured of a chronic physical condition. We got rid of the sofa bed when we moved . . . just in case he showed up on the doorstep of our new place.

Gruel

½ cup amaranth
1½ cups water
¼ cup unsweetened almond milk
no salt
1 teaspoon flaxseed oil
1 teaspoon hempseed
1 scant tablespoon whole milk yogurt, preferably
   expired
1 teaspoon whey powder

1. Combine amaranth, water, and almond milk in a small saucepan.
2. Bring to a boil. Reduce heat and cover.
3. Cook for 30 to 40 minutes, not stirring frequently enough to prevent amaranth from forming a thick crust on the bottom and sides of pan.
4. Remove from heat. Scrape contents into a bowl and stir in remaining ingredients.
   Half-fill pot with water and leave in sink.

Serves: you right if you eat this.

is for

Huitlacoche

After a particularly trying day of working with Josefina
Howard on her culinary autobiography, I sometimes
turned for solace to David Plante's *Difficult Women*, a tri-
partite memoir of his relationships with Jean Rhys, Sonia
Orwell, and Germaine Greer. I felt a perversely soothing
schadenfreude at Plante's horror in accidentally wedging
the elderly, drunken Rhys into a toilet bowl; nothing
shrank Josefina's outsized ego like reading of how Plante
arrived for a long stay at Greer's isolated Tuscan farmhouse
to hear her bellowing at another guest's baby, "That's not
the way to use fucking finger paints!" A friend who has
been a successful editor for more than fifty years is fond of

saying, "Books are like children: you can never do enough for them." Every time he says it, I mentally replace "books" with "authors," which is why he has lasted in the business for more than half a century, whereas I left with an anxiety disorder after a decade. And while I wasn't thinking of Plante as I sneaked the final pages of Josefina's manuscript into my bag while paramedics strapped her onto a stretcher, it is just the sort of thing he might have written about. Difficult women provoke desperate behavior.

Josefina was often referred to as "a force of nature," a phrase that captures the inhuman quality of those willing to flatten entire cities to get what they want. Invariably, such people are more fun to read about than to know. Nevertheless, a woman doesn't merit the label "difficult" unless her outrageousness is counterbalanced by some hugely positive quality. Josefina's was her missionary zeal for the cuisine of her adoptive country. Although born in Cuba and raised in Spain, no one was more passionate about the food of Mexico. When she opened Rosa Mexicano on the Upper East Side in 1984, authentic Mexican cooking was all but unknown in New York City, and she was almost single-handedly responsible for introducing the authentic flavors of the country to a group of diners who were hungry for it.

Seven nights a week for more than fifteen years, Josefina held court from the same table, monitoring the room from a throne-like chair whose carved wooden back rose above her head in a dark crescent, gray hair swept back from her forehead, eyes steely under straight black brows. If she spotted a lapse, she would teleport to correct it, vanishing before your eyes. She did not make the rounds like many owners, visiting the tables of VIPs and regulars; patrons stopped by and paid their respects to her, always addressing her as Mrs. Howard. Those not in the know sometimes called her Rosa, summoning thunderclouds in her face. Worse still, they occasionally had the audacity to suggest that the spelling of the restaurant should be corrected— to "Mexicana"—to reflect agreement between the noun and adjective: Rosa's Mexican restaurant. Josefina would explain with exaggerated courtesy that "Rosa Mexicano" refers to the shade of Mexican pink that embodies the heart of the country: Elsa Schiaparelli's shocking pink, the pulsing color of bougainvillea, a few degrees hotter than magenta, the hue even of the Mexican taxis. I always suspected the restaurant would be fully booked the next time they called for a reservation.

One night I slid into the chair opposite her. I was a cookbook editor, and the marketing director had told me to march in there and get Mrs. Howard to sign a contract, which editors and agents had been trying to do for years. Like a lot of powerful people, Josefina had devised a uniform for public life, which she was wearing that first evening we met: a bright, loose-fitting silk shirt over black pants. Only the most stylish women can make the absence of jewelry a statement, and I could almost see the ghost of Mexican silver at her wrists and throat. As we started to talk, Josefina told me she had never found anyone who understood her well enough to tell her story. The last editor had been thrown out on her ear because she hadn't known who Noël Coward was.

"Can you imagine?" Josefina barked incredulously, shaking her handsome gray head. "'Out!' I said to her. 'Get out of my restaurant!' At first, she didn't believe me, but I was serious."

Luckily for me—or, as I thought later, perhaps not— she and I saw eye to eye despite my not knowing Spanish and never having visited Mexico. After years of saying no, she signed a book contract. Perhaps I just caught her at the right time. She was getting on in years, although her ageless face made it impossible to tell exactly how old she was, and woe betide the person who asked her.

From that evening on, she began to seduce me with food. It was more than an education: it was an indoctrination into the cult of Josefina's Mexico. It was her spiritual homeland, and she had the gift of communicating its essence precisely because it was not native to her. The closest I can come to describing the experience is to say it was like falling in love, not with her, but with the country

I had never seen, through its food. Even now, after having visited Mexico, I look back on that time as if the country and I had an affair—brief, intense, colorful, full of new flavors and savors and excitements, and then abruptly over. People are always surprised—I am still surprised myself—at the depth of my understanding of Mexican cuisine, its influences and evolution. All of this she managed to convey in about nine months.

Here is what I remember. Not the pomegranate margaritas, although they were clearly a preoccupation for Martha Stewart when she had Josefina on her show multiple times (I was a little embarrassed for Martha about that). Josefina was quite insulted when people ruined her food by drinking margaritas during the meal. I remember her asking huffily (not to their faces, of course; even she wouldn't do that), "Would people drink margaritas during a French meal? An Italian one?" I do remember being offered a shot of good tequila followed by a chaser of *sangrita*, an elegant cylindrical shot glass of pomegranate and bitter orange juice served chilled as an aperitif. This might be followed, in season, by a tiny cup of *esquites*, young sweet corn kernels barely sautéed in butter and serrano chile and flavored with chopped epazote. Ah yes, those herbs: fresh epazote, hard to find, with its seductively stinky aroma of petroleum and citrus. Sharp, soapy cilantro (which she pronounced see-LAN-tro, with a tender elongation of the first syllable and a rolling of the "r"—she had a smoky, beautiful voice whose rich timbre sometimes vibrated with a mysterious purr). And *hoya santa*, whose huge leaves smelled like sassafras and black pepper. Even now, crumbling a few dried leaves and stems can call up, like the scent of a faded wedding bouquet, a ghostly parade of exciting dishes from the kitchen. I can see Josefina's strong, ringless fingers offering me a small tortilla, still warm, rolled around some savory tidbit she wanted me to try. Josefina always wanted me to taste something or other, but she would never offer it on a cold metal fork. It is very intimate to accept food from someone's fingers, and I remember how gently she handed me those tortillas, as if she were conveying gifts that she didn't want to bruise. They could be filled with anything—the house's famous guacamole, made tableside in a *molcajete* that could have been lifted from the Museum of Natural History—or my favorite dish, Mixiotes de Cordero. These lamb shanks, coated with chiles, garlic, and spice, were wrapped in a tall parchment bundle that would arrive at the table straight from the oven. When the waiter unwrapped it with a flourish, a billow of fragrant steam would envelop your face. Wrapping the meltingly tender shreds of lamb in a tortilla and mopping it in the puddle of pungent juices that had collected in the parchment below was one of the culinary high points of my life.

I remember the first time I tasted her red, white, and green *chiles en nogada*, the delicate heat of the chiles offset by the creamy white sauce and punctuated with the astringent burst of pomegranate arils. She introduced me to elaborate, complicated moles and to the bright, sophisticated seafood dishes of Veracruz. One bitter cold evening, when I arrived at the restaurant feeling chilled to the bone and utterly depleted, Josefina put before me a bowl of pozole, the iconic pork and hominy stew. After telling me it was made from pig's heads and feet, she waited expectantly for me to dig in. I had no choice, but it took only a few delicious bites to banish all thoughts of its dubious origins. By the time I left, I felt atavistically fortified by generations of Mexican women and ready to face life again.

Josefina's uncompromising quest to bring new flavors and ingredients to the restaurant brought her into near-constant conflict with her partners, who were more concerned with the bottom line than with authenticity. Her battles with these five men were epic and bloody. In today's adventurous climate, where a Lower East Side "New Mexican" restaurant can put dried earthworms in a dessert and toasted grasshopper tacos with ant-salt guacamole don't cause anyone to blink an eye, it is hard to fathom what a struggle it was for her to serve *huitlacoche* at Rosa Mexicano. Known in English as "corn smut," *huitlacoche* is a fungus that causes the ear of corn to swell enormously and turn black, bursting out of the husk. Despite its disgusting appearance, it has a delicious flavor when cooked—delicate and mushroom-like with a sweet hint of corn. The word derives from Nahuatl for "black excrement," but *huitlacoche* tastes so heavenly that it is sometimes known as the "excrement of the gods," an epithet that captures the unique ambivalence aroused by something that tastes so good while looking so repulsive. At Rosa Mexicano, *huitlacoche* was folded into a crepe with creamy mascarpone and manchego cheese—and always seasoned with epazote, with which Josefina believed it had an almost symbiotic relationship. Although she never won her long-running battle to introduce ants to her customers, she prevailed in creating an ever-evolving menu whose excitement kept them coming back year after year.

Despite her indomitability, Josefina carried an indefinable aura of tragedy. Even though she was writing an autobiography, she never brought up her past. Only from the final manuscript did I learn that she became a war refugee as a child after her father and grandmother were assassinated by opposing sides in the Spanish Civil War. I'd had no idea of the years of struggle and poverty she and her mother endured, only the bare outlines of which she shared in the manuscript. Saddest of all was the single sentence where she conveyed that one of her sons had died. And yet the ultimate message was that she had worked hard all her life, had her loves, her friends, her successes, her adventures. A remarkably resilient life then—a full life—if not exactly a happy one.

Josefina wanted her book to capture the magic of Mexico as her restaurant had, but she wasn't a writer, a limitation compounded by the fact that English was not her native language. She had been recounting anecdotes for so many years that she thought it would be a cinch to transfer them to the page, but she soon discovered that writing and talking are not the same thing. Furthermore, she had waited so long to tell her story that the freight of her ambitions multiplied; over the years, the load of what she wanted to convey had taken on impossible proportions. Writing was agonizing, so it was easier to procrastinate, complain, blame, prevaricate, and create complications. Finally, she hired a friend to help her. Usually, this is a recipe for disaster, but luckily it worked. Unfortunately, Lila Lomeli wrote in Spanish, so we needed to hire a translator. Then there were recipes to be transcribed and tested, because Josefina was also not a chef. She had particularly high aspirations for the book's appearance, since she had been a professional interior designer before becoming a restaurateur. In addition to agonizing over the photographs and illustrations, she had strong opinions on color, typeface, endpapers. The book was postponed once, missing the Christmas catalog, and then again. I was eight months pregnant by this point, and one day my boss informed me that I had until Friday to transmit the manuscript, or else. I did not want to find out what "or else" meant two weeks before going on maternity leave.

The book was essentially finished, but Josefina had been holed up at home fussing with the final pages for more than a week. It looked like I would have to go to her apartment to get it. Although she claimed to be ill, I was certain she was only suffering from a severe case of completion anxiety. She didn't answer when I phoned to say I'd be coming over after work, and it took her a full five minutes to respond to my insistent buzzing on the intercom. When she finally pressed the button, her voice crackled weakly that I couldn't come up because she wasn't dressed, but I insisted.

I was taken aback by the old woman who opened the door. All the color had been leached out of her—not only from her ashen skin but also her flattened hair and rumpled clothes. As I followed her into the stuffy living room, I was surprised by an odor of unwashed linens and something more troubling, an undertone of decay that I would recognize only later in life as a sign of serious illness. While I still believed her illness was psychosomatic, I felt a sharp twinge of fear: this breakdown went far beyond completion anxiety. At the same time, I couldn't help being thoroughly disconcerted by her apartment. It wasn't the considerable mess that bothered me but the utter impersonality of the place. Where were the artifacts from her travels, the mementos and photographs, the rich detritus of a life well lived that Rosa Mexicano had led me to expect? This featureless box could have been a sample unit for a management company, or a fake room in the furniture department at Bloomingdale's. It made me wonder which was the real Josefina, the stranger who apparently lived here or the one I knew, who presided over the restaurant every night. Was Josefina's larger-than-life persona a vampire that fed on her private life, leaving only this husk behind?

The round white dining table, which looked as if it had never seen a meal, was scattered with manuscript pages, and I thought it was in her interest as well as mine to get them out of her hands. We had just started to go through the few remaining queries when Josefina began to complain of leg cramps and went to lie down on the sofa. I was wondering what to do when I heard groans from the living room. Clearly in agony, she wouldn't allow me to call her doctor (she said she didn't have one) or her son (she didn't want to bother him). Finally, over her strenuous objections, I dialed 911. As the paramedics lifted her onto a stretcher, I surreptitiously stuffed the loose pages into my satchel. Maybe her baby could wait to come into the world, but mine couldn't.

On the way to the emergency room, I called my doctor to see if she could recommend a colleague at the hospital. Although Josefina's condition was not diagnosed that evening, the pains in her legs were caused by blood clots, one of which would break off four months later and lodge in her brain, causing a massive stroke. She would live for six more years, but she would never speak again.

Josefina's stroke occurred while I was on maternity leave, and I didn't learn of it until I returned to work several months later. I kept telling myself that I should go visit her, but I didn't. I thought it was because I had a new baby and a demanding job, but I realize now that on some level I felt guilty for pushing her to finish the book and partly responsible for what happened to her. Intellectually, I don't believe she would have lived longer if I had allowed her to leave those pages on the dining table as the weeks turned into months or even years, but the heart believes what it believes. It is an ironic consolation that her book was published three months after she was robbed of the ability to tell her story. Sometimes I imagine her, in her long silence, handing the glossy volume to visitors, having at least the satisfaction that it will tell them exactly what she wants them to know of her life and no more.

Crepes Filled with Huitlacoche, Gratinéed with Mascarpone and Manchego Cheese

(from *Rosa Mexicano: A Culinary Autobiography with 60 Recipes* by Josefina Howard)

On the page before this recipe appears, Josefina appends the following footnote to the "All-Huitlacoche Dinner" she prepared for the James Beard Foundation: "Cuitlacoche can also be spelled huitlacoche." Since huitlacoche is the preferred spelling, I took the liberty of changing it in this recipe.

Crepes:

  2 cups milk

  5 large eggs

  1 pinch each of sugar and salt

  2 ounces flour

  2 ounces butter, melted

  ¼ pound butter, clarified

1. In a medium-sized bowl, whisk the milk, eggs, sugar, and salt. Sift the flour into another bowl, add a little of the liquid, and stir to make a paste. Incorporate the

rest of the liquid and the melted butter, and mix just enough to combine. If there are lumps of flour, strain through a fine sieve. Allow the batter to sit for ½ hour before using or, for best results, overnight.

2. In a nonstick pan or 6-inch sauté pan, melt ½ tablespoon of the clarified butter over low to medium heat. Tilt the pan to coat the surface with the butter and pour out any excess. Ladle approximately 2 tablespoons of the crepe mixture into the pan. Quickly rotate the pan so the mixture evenly covers the bottom. Cook for 1 to 1½ minutes and gently flip with a spatula, being careful not to tear the crepe. Cook for 30 to 45 seconds and remove from the pan. Repeat the process until the batter is finished. Stack the crepes on a plate and cover with a kitchen towel.

Huitlacoche filling:

3 tablespoons vegetable oil

2 tablespoons butter

½ medium white onion, chopped

1 garlic clove, finely chopped

1 serrano chile, seeded and very finely chopped

1½ pound huitlacoche, frozen or canned

¾ cup small kernels of corn, fresh or frozen

salt to taste

2 tablespoons chopped epazote

Garnish:

4½ ounces mascarpone cheese

4½ ounces manchego cheese, grated

small leaves of epazote, for garnish

1. Heat the vegetable oil and butter in a 10-inch sauté pan. Sauté the onion for 4 to 5 minutes, add the garlic, and cook over medium heat until the onions are translucent. Add the chile, huitlacoche, corn, and salt, and cook until most of the liquid has evaporated. Stir in the chopped epazote; set aside to cool.
2. Place 2 to 3 tablespoons of the huitlacoche filling across the center of the crepes. Roll the crepes and place 3 on each plate, seam side down.
3. Place approximately 1½ tablespoons mascarpone cheese on top of each plate of crepes and sprinkle with 1½ tablespoons manchego cheese.
4. Place under the salamander or broiler to heat and melt the cheese. Garnish with the epazote leaves.

Serves: 6

Note: Mascarpone cheese is substituted for the clotted cream or triple cream found in Mexico.

is for

Indian Breakfast

Our trip to Rajasthan was born promisingly enough, with a tipsy bid at a silent auction on a package called "Stay at the Taj Mahal." The description read like an opium dream, the cities themselves an incantation: Jaipur, Jodhpur, Udaipur. Half-believing the minimum bid to be missing a zero and certain the competition would be fierce, we gave only a pro forma glance at the sheet as we were leaving. Our name was the only one there. We were thrilled until we actually began planning the trip, when the gap between fantasy and reality threatened to swallow us whole. By the time we left on separate airlines—to ensure that our seven-year-old would not be left an orphan in case of a plane crash—we were barely speaking.

How to explain, then, the almost queasy joy I felt on spotting my husband's face across a sea of heads in the fluorescent chaos of baggage claim in Delhi? Somehow, an improbable confluence of delays on behalf of both airlines had resulted in our arriving within moments instead of hours of each other. I was so weak-kneed with relief at not having to pretend to be brave about making my way to a hotel on my own in the middle of the night that I stepped effortlessly into an alternate dimension where it was easy to remember having swapped traveler's tales a decade ago with the attractive man across the carousel. What exactly had I found so irritating about him the day before? It was like trying to locate a word I couldn't quite remember. I felt as if the universe itself had colluded in our reconciliation, and the spell did not wear off during a glorious week and a half.

Now, the night before our departure, the pièce de résistance: we were about to have drinks with the maharana of Udaipur. When we stepped off the little launch from the Lake Palace Hotel, the driveway was empty, although the palace had said it would send a car. My husband informed the brocaded dock attendants, who exchanged a quizzical look before the senior one made a hurried phone call, and a few moments later a venerable black Ambassador rolled up, emblazoned with the royal Mewar coat of arms. Humiliating as it was to arrive at the door a mere fifty yards away, I was grateful to have been spared the larger embarrassment of wandering around looking for the entrance—rather modest as palace entrances go. I still hadn't recovered from the only other time I'd been invited to visit the aristocracy, when I drove up to the rear of a Loire chateau and mistook my host for the gardener, watching his amused expression curdle into horrified disbelief as my French deteriorated into complete gibberish.

We were greeted by Jyoti Jasol, who was to the maharana of Udaipur what Condoleezza Rice had been to George W. Bush—a sort of official "wife." Gorgeous and statuesque, she resembled the court ladies in Indian miniature paintings. Her sari was made of an exquisite silk chiffon edged in silver, of a turquoise so intensely saturated it seemed impossible that a fabric could possibly hold that much color. In all the riotous panoply of color I saw in the saris of Rajasthan, hers was the only blue one. Looking at her elegant silhouette and graceful head wrap, I was suddenly, painfully conscious of my bare knees. The day we arrived, our guide had told us that in India only Muslim women wear black, thus rendering most of my evening clothes unsuitable. Luckily, at the last moment I had remembered the great Diana Vreeland's dictum, "Pink is the navy blue of India," and had decided to throw a short floral shift into my suitcase. As a few other guests drifted in wearing khaki and linen, I wished I had trusted the "smart casual" on the invitation. Feeling at once overdressed and overexposed, I envied my husband his impeccable suit.

Jyoti led us down a brightly lit gallery with tantalizing rooms opening out on either side—too fast to peek—onto a moonlit terrace, saying that the maharana used it as a sort of outdoor office. Tapestried chairs were arranged in an oval on an exquisite carpet in the center of a lawn, truly a luxury in desert Rajasthan. Five of the other six guests were connected with a factory recently established in Udaipur by Odegard, a high-end carpet manufacturer. The sixth was a French journalist. There was an awkward silence as we stood waiting for the maharana, whom we were told to call by the affectionate honorific "Shri Ji." Although we were on the lookout for him, he managed somehow to materialize unobserved from a hidden door. A stout gray-bearded man in his early sixties with deep pouches under his eyes, wearing sandals and a short-sleeved shirt with many pockets, he gave an impression of power and congestion, like the late Orson Welles playing a nineteenth-century English explorer. He muttered a vague general greeting and waved me to a chair on his left. Forty years of Western woman autopilot kicked in, and only the lightning-quick hand of my husband prevented my derriere from performing the enormous gaffe of landing on its chair before His Highness's reached his. *I owe you one*, I thought gratefully. Servants emerged from the shadows bearing silver trays. His Highness sat down heavily. "There's wine and fruit juice for those of you who don't want spirits," he said, pronouncing it "spidits" like a character in a British drawing room comedy. I thought I caught a note of wistfulness in his voice as he said it, so when the first tray came my way I asked if any of the glasses held Scotch. "Any of the four in the center," he said with his first show of enthusiasm. "At last, I've found someone to drink Scotch with me!" I felt sorry for throwing the servant into a tizzy, though, by taking it with only water, not ice and soda as the maharana did. Another gaffe.

While drinks were served and he chatted with the head designer of Odegard, a smooth dude from Williamsburg, Brooklyn, obviously a favorite, I got an opportunity to observe him. I saw no trace of the disciplined polo player he had been, although I already liked him well enough to be glad he had escaped the tragic toll that sport had taken on so many Rajput princes. Just days before, we had seen the young maharana of neighboring Jodhpur, crippled in a match the previous year, haunting the Trophy Bar of the monstrously overgrown and nearly deserted Umaid Bhawan Palace. The impression of heaviness Shri

Ji conveyed seemed to be spiritual as much as physical. We had heard during our tour of the City Palace earlier that day that his father had become a "king without a kingdom" in 1970 when Indira Gandhi cut off his privy purse. When Shri Ji became the seventy-sixth scion of a Rajput dynasty founded in 734 AD, he found himself in the unenviable position of trying to provide for the people of Udaipur without the means to do so.

The wind kicked up, and Jyoti shielded her face prettily with her *orhni*, a long swath of the same turquoise silk as her sari. She and the maharana briefly discussed and dismissed moving inside. The company's limited store of small talk was beginning to sputter, and she looked at me expectantly. Seated at the left hand of the maharana, I was clearly expected to sing for my Scotch, but my mind obdurately refused to produce. I surreptitiously slid my notebook out of my evening bag, but to my horror I found everyone staring at me in silence to see what jewel it would produce. The questions I had hastily scribbled in the hotel room now seemed embarrassingly banal. Why hadn't I listened to my husband and done more homework? I felt my face turn scarlet and hoped it was too dark for anyone to notice. Jyoti darted me a reproachful glance. The maharana gave up and turned back to Mr. Williamsburg.

He was certainly a powerful personality. Was it boredom he was emanating? Impatience? Loneliness? No, that wasn't quite it. He seemed utterly, unimaginably alone in a way that was impervious to human companionship. Like Ishi stumbling out of the forest, he was the last of his breed, the end of the line. Even if there were a few maharanas left in name, he was the only real thing, trying to hold on to some measure of power and wealth through the exercise of sheer will and wits, as a canny hotelier, among other things, which was why I was here. And I couldn't even think of a single intelligent question to ask him.

My shame-filled musings were interrupted by my husband's voice. "Your Highness," he began, "I've been reading about your policy of self-reliance and self-respect. . . ." I was so flooded with relief that I stopped hearing his voice. My eyes mindlessly followed the bats circling and dipping overhead in their disconcertingly sudden way until my attention was jerked back to the conversation by the welcome sound of the maharana's laughter. "What have you been reading?" he boomed. "You're an encyclopedia!"

In addition to devouring several guidebooks and paying better attention than I that afternoon to our marvelously overeducated guide, my husband had been reading the *New York Times* front to back for the past thirty years. By now he and the maharana were deep into a discussion of solar energy, one of His Highness's passions and one of my husband's former professions. Diplomatically suggesting that solar energy might not be the solution to India's energy problems, my husband explained why he had turned to wind energy, and our gathering suddenly ceased to be a cocktail party. Shri Ji waved his hand majestically for him to continue, transformed into Yul Brynner in *The King and I*. If not for the two cell phones on the table, we could easily have time-traveled back a millennium. My husband clearly had the king's ear. To his credit, he rose to the occasion, delivering a brilliant soliloquy that began with Apple Computer's hammer and sickle ad at the Super Bowl in 1984—"an important year for you, Your Highness" (how had he remembered his coronation year?)—and somehow segued into Udaipur as a potential role model for India's energy future. Jyoti beamed; the group seemed to let out a collective sigh of relief. I decided it was safe to have another Scotch (when the poor servant put ice in it by mistake, I saw the evening's only flash of royal anger, as if a tiger had leapt from the shadows). As we were leaving, Shri Ji invited us to his birthday celebration in December, and I felt a rush of gratitude and admiration for my husband, who must have been a courtier in a former life.

I opened my eyes the next morning pleasantly disoriented and as well-rested as a child. It was not that I didn't recall where I was—our exquisite little room at the Lake Palace

Hotel was unmistakable in the delicate predawn light. It was myself that felt unfamiliar. The anxiety and dread that had greeted me every morning for as long as I could remember were absent. I was like a convalescent who suddenly awakens without pain. I briefly recalled the previous evening, a nightmare that had morphed into a good dream because of the man who, like a spouse in a post-code Hollywood movie, was lying in the other twin bed. But I felt too energetic to stay in bed and ruminate. Determined not to wake him, I dressed silently and slipped out into the corridor, at the end of which a door opened onto a white marble courtyard terrace.

The lake in the moments just before sunrise was as nacreous as the inside of a huge oyster shell. Flocks of pigeons wheeled gustily around my head, and I ducked beneath a carved lintel to escape the fate of the marble *putti* dotting the terrace. From my sheltered vantage point, I looked out over the water toward the City Palace and the Shiv Niwas, where we had had drinks the night before. Taking my first deep breath in more than a week, I realized that this was my first moment alone since I had left New York ten days earlier. At every doorway, around every corner, lurked a silent factotum in a snowy kurta and fabulous turban for whom my every wish was a command—to the point where I had to be careful what I wished for. For the tourist in India, privacy—not service—is the great luxury.

As the sun inched over the horizon, its glow warmed the domes of the Jag Mandir across the water and revealed it to be of yellow sandstone rather than marble, transforming it so completely that I had to blink to convince myself it was the same building. Graceful chalk-white terns and stiff-winged sandpipers skimmed across the lake, and something that looked like an enormous black butterfly flittered bare inches above the surface, buffeted by invisible currents in the motionless air. From the shore rose the barking, crowing, and raucous mewling of the ubiquitous wild peacock (India's national bird), whose call, like an alley cat in heat, is as ugly as its plumage is beautiful. As the wind freshened, my stomach reminded me that I hadn't eaten since a delicious lunch the day before, a palace burger made of lamb and cilantro with mango pickle.

Since I was the first customer in the restaurant, I was seated at a corner table with a double view of the lake. As I spread my napkin over my lap, the waiter courteously pointed out the English breakfast buffet, typical of a good hotel anywhere in the world. When I asked if there was a local breakfast available, he smiled and pointed to a single item at the bottom of the enormous leather menu. Poori bhaji was not exactly a local specialty, he explained. Although it was now found all over the country, the deep-fried puffy bread served with a potato curry was of Southern origin. It was close enough for me. From the moment I dunked a croissant into a real café au lait in a Paris hotel room at seventeen, I realized that eating the native breakfast is one of the few foolproof ways to communicate to your body that you have actually left home. Nothing calls up Mexico for me like the memory of chilaquiles, Germany like vast platters of cold meats, Venezuela like silky passion fruit juice . . .

Fortified with a pot of French press coffee, I watched the lake assume its daytime persona in the sun's glare off the water. The waiter reappeared with a silver tray, lifting its domed cover to reveal four puffy, golden poori. Blistered and glistening with oil, they looked like inflated blowfish pulled straight from the water. Next to them sat a bowl of marigold-colored potato curry, flecked with bright green cilantro leaves and studded with black mustard seeds. Two tiny dishes completed the tableau, one containing a mixture of freshly chopped green chiles, onion, and cilantro, the other a potent-looking paste of red chiles. I picked up and promptly dropped a scalding poori. While I waited for it to cool, I tasted the potatoes. "Mouth-watering" has been drained of significance by overuse, but in that moment I experienced its literal meaning. The bhaji, essentially a dry potato curry, was so delicious that my heart began pounding with anxiety at the thought that soon it would be gone. First it was tangy verging on sour, like sorrel soup, then spicy, then salty. Next came the bite of mustard seeds, the astringency of ginger, the reassuring warmth of garlic, the sweetness of caramelized onions, and an alluringly musky spice I couldn't place but now believe was *hing*, or asafetida. The poori was now cool enough to touch, and I ripped off the edge. A breath of warm air rushed out, and it deflated in my hand like a living thing. The combination of the poori and the bhaji was indescribable. I tried to make it last as long as I could by experimenting with various combinations of the condiments on the table, but inevitably everything disappeared except some of the fiery pepper paste. When the waiter removed the empty tray, I was too satisfied to feel sorry.

is for

Jordan Almonds

It's been twenty-five years, and I still haven't recovered from the inexplicable disappearance of Jordan almonds from movie theater concession stands. Ridiculous, I know, but some foods and activities are like Siamese twins, bound together so intimately that separating them does irreparable harm to both. Going to the movies just isn't the same without Jordan almonds. And it doesn't work to smuggle them in from outside; I've tried it. They taste different when not warmed by the lamps of the concession stand.

Like most children, I spent my formative years at the movies consuming tubs of buttered popcorn, Raisinets, Good & Plenty, and Whoppers. I didn't discover Jordan almonds until I was fifteen, at the same moment I discovered "cinema." Both seemed equally adult to me. Serious film—which for me included everything from Woody Allen to Lina Wertmüller—gave me the key to making sense of the adult world and, although the people on the screen were actors, I saw them as visible proof that the complex, exciting people I fantasized about truly existed.

Most of all, these films provided a psychic escape from Trevose, Pennsylvania, a suburb so lacking in identity that it is classified a "census-designated place" rather than a town. Trevose could easily have been the subject of Gertrude Stein's famous pronouncement, "there's no there there." If for some peculiar reason you were to go on TripAdvisor searching for a dining recommendation, you would find, in order of preference, an Italian restaurant, Cracker Barrel, and—almost too perfect to be true—the Suburban Diner Restaurant on West Street Road. The problem with the Trevoses of the world is not that most people don't seem to mind living in them. It is that they mind that you mind.

The nearest place to find some relief before I left for college (and forever) was Philadelphia, which in the seventies was a vast agglomeration of neighborhoods with a tiny nucleus at its center, fittingly called "Center City." In that miniature urban oasis, there was an even smaller section, called South Street—perhaps seven blocks long by three wide—that had a bit of the edgy pioneer energy that teenagers find so intoxicating. Every weekend I took the commuter train from Suburban Station to gawk surreptitiously at the embryonic punk fashion scene (although I was often too cowed to actually walk into the stores) and wander through the art museums. But what really drew me to Philadelphia weekend after weekend were two movie theaters: the Theatre of Living Arts, known as TLA, and the Ritz.

Mecca for me was TLA, a gritty cinema on South and 3rd Streets that showed a truly impressive roster of repertory, foreign, and cult films. I can still feel my hand smoothing out the folds of the enormous quarterly schedule on my bedroom's hot pink shag rug. I would kneel until my back ached and my knees were numb, poring over the titles and thumbnail descriptions, planning my Saturday expeditions like Peary to the North Pole. In the days before videos, DVDs, and streaming, the only way to see the "canon" was to go the movies, and during my high school years—guided by books of film criticism by John Simon and Pauline Kael—I saw an eclectic array of films by directors like Bergman, Fellini, Truffaut, Cassavetes, Herzog, Ken Russell, and Volker Schlöndorff, mixed with lighter fare by Busby Berkeley, Preston Sturges, and Billy Wilder. Less often, I went to the Ritz in tony Society Hill to keep up with current "art" and foreign films.

My Saturday afternoons at the movies were sacred, and everything about them was ritualized. I had to arrive early not only because Alvy Singer, Woody Allen's character in *Annie Hall,* refused to go into the four-and-a-half-hour screening of *The Sorrow and the Pity* because he missed the first few seconds of the credits but also because I needed to buy Jordan almonds from the concession stand. At TLA, I always tried to sit in the fourth row center, or as close to it as I could get, so that I could put my feet up on the seat in front of me (there were no ushers to prevent you) and no head would block my view. The black upholstered seats were stained and torn, some entirely broken, some crazily tilted, so you had to move along the row until, like Goldilocks, you found one that was just right. I still remember the excitingly unwholesome smell of that dilapidated theater, left over from the notorious midnight screening of *The Rocky Horror Picture Show* just hours before. Nearly everyone went alone on Saturday afternoon; the point was not socializing but seeing the films. I'm sure that my enduring preference for going to the movies by myself stems from those early days.

I don't remember exactly when I first tasted Jordan almonds, but their somewhat elusive appeal seemed perfect for the often disturbing and ambiguous films I had started seeing. Unlike the simple sweetness of Raisinets or Whoppers, the confectionary equivalent of what was shown in suburban multiplexes, the Jordan almonds of that time had a soapy quality, a touch of perfume. Like everything else that adults seemed to prefer—gin or broccoli rabe or black coffee—they were an acquired taste, and I was determined to acquire it.

Stringent and inviolable rules governed the consumption of Jordan almonds. Rule number one: if I was seeing one movie, I bought one box; a double feature, two boxes. Rule number two: no matter how hungry I was, I could not begin eating them until the credits began to roll. Rule number three: it was necessary to suck on the shell in such a way as to ensure a uniform thinness all around, flipping the almond as necessary. The sugar coating never became rough and grainy during the process as it sometimes does with the Jordan almonds of today, which can abrade your tongue like sandpaper. After losing their initial slick coating, they retained their satiny texture as the shell became thinner, until the barest hint of the woody almond beneath could be detected. At that moment, while a hint of resistance remained, it was time to *crunch* down, creating an explosion of slightly bitter almond and a rush of sugar.

Watching a movie with subtitles while engaging with a box of Jordan almonds is a wholly immersive experience, requiring complete concentration to focus simultaneously on the story, the camerawork, the spoken language, the subtitles (especially in the case of Romance languages, where you can try to figure out the translation), and the tricky business of getting the shell to just the right thinness before biting down. Sometimes at key plot points I would lose track and end up with a naked, mealy almond in my mouth or, conversely, during a crisis, find myself mindlessly crunching through a handful of candies, leaving myself short during the remainder of the movie. During stretches of excruciating boredom, I would conduct blind taste tests to see if there was a difference in flavor between the various colors. For example, while suffering through *The Tree of Wooden Clogs*—an Ermanno Olmi film so excruciatingly slow that the seasons seem to change on the screen in real time—I discovered there was a subtle hint of extra vanilla in the white ones.

Jordan almonds disappeared from movie theaters sometime in the mid-1980s—first spottily, then completely. For me they are frozen in a certain era of movie-going, when I was open to everything and when I sought and found in the darkened theater not mere escape, but transport.

is for

Kielbasa

The universe of food when I was growing up was divided into three Dantean realms: heaven, purgatory, and hell. Heaven corresponded to my grandmother's kitchen, where the vegetables were fresh and prepared in surprising but always delicious ways. Purgatory was the dinner table at home, where my mother served boiled frozen lima beans, frozen broccoli florets, and frozen serrated carrot coins, which she supplemented with the occasional head of iceberg lettuce. And hell was my father's house, the land of the can. This culinary cosmology makes sense to me now: my grandmother was an Italian cook, my mother a product of American supermarket culture, and my father a peculiar Polish American bachelor hybrid. But at the time I merely dreaded having to eat there during my weekly Saturday visitation.

My father subsisted on a diet of instant Sanka, menthol cigarettes, and buttermilk (for his ulcers). For lunch, he served either canned potato soup or sardines on Saltines. It is easy to imagine the horror these meals inspired in a child. On Saturday nights he made pot roast, blasted so long in the pressure cooker that it fell apart into matchsticks that stuck to your teeth. This was invariably accompanied by watery canned "French" green beans and the only edible dish, mashed potatoes with buttermilk. Only rarely did I stay over; he liked to watch the *Creature Features* after I went to bed, and the sound of the opening scream traveled up the stairs to my room and terrified me. When I did, though, he would boil a thick, U-shaped kielbasa for Sunday breakfast, steaming up the small kitchen with a delicious, garlicky fog. After draining the sausage, he would fry the slices with some scrambled eggs, which tasted doubly good because I was so hungry from the day before.

Perhaps for this reason, I remain inordinately fond of kielbasa, which he pronounced "kel-bassy." Its charms are best displayed in white borscht—the best soup in the world, in my humble opinion. I first discovered it at a now defunct Polish coffee shop in the East Village called Angelica's, not to be confused with the well-known vegan restaurant of that name. Angelica's was famous for its soups, of which it served a rotating variety every day. It was late on a frigid Saturday afternoon when I slid onto a stool at the lunch counter, chilled to the bone because the March sun that morning had tricked me into dressing prematurely for spring. I'm not sure why I ordered the white borscht; probably I expected it to have something in common with its red cousin. It's just as well I didn't know that the white variety is based on sauerkraut and contains no beets at all, or I might have chosen something else. A steaming bowl appeared before me almost instantly, brimming with a nearly opaque white broth flecked with herbs. Slices of kielbasa could be spied floating just beneath the surface. The sharp tanginess of the first spoonful was a wonderful shock, tempered by the soup's creamy texture and punctuated by discs of chewy, smoky meat. There was a primal reassurance in the warmth that spread through my limbs. Hands down, it was the best soup I had ever eaten.

I remained so enamored of white borscht that, ten years after that first bowlful, I impulsively decided to take a winter vacation to Cracow for the sole purpose of eating it at the source twice a day for a week. As soon as I had checked into my hotel, I wandered over to a nearby restaurant to begin my white borscht fest. It was not on the menu. Screwing up my courage to ask the waiter, I received a look of polite incomprehension. I assumed this was a fluke until the experience was repeated in every restaurant during the next three or four days. Increasingly disappointed and puzzled, I concluded that white borscht must be one of those home-cooked dishes that aren't deemed worthy of serious restaurants and sought out some real holes-in-the-wall. Still no luck.

Meanwhile, it snowed. Not Manhattan snow, festive and clean, muffling sharp edges and hiding dirt and then disappearing. Cracow snow fell silent and inexorable from a windless sky, continuing ceaselessly day into night into day until it threatened to erase the world. My trip was turning into a terrible mistake. Then one day, when the flakes had turned to freezing rain and the streets to slush that seeped into my boots, I stopped in a subterranean tourist restaurant next to Ripley's Believe It or Not. I was ushered past a long bar to a heavy wooden table in the back room. Flipping through the laminated pages of the menu, badly translated into four languages, I saw it! To be polite, I also ordered a drink and an appetizer, but I could hardly contain my excitement and relief. My visit had been redeemed, my judgment vindicated.

The drink and appetizer arrived promptly, but the soup did not. I waited. The couple on my left finished their meal, had coffee, and left. A large family in the corner ordered lunch and were served. I motioned for the waiter and asked where my soup was. He gave me a blank stare

and disappeared into the kitchen. The family started in on dessert. I began to feel paranoid as well as hungry. Was it my imagination or were the waiters furtively whispering to each other about me? Was I being singled out for ill treatment because I was a woman eating alone? Finally, feeling desperate, I scraped my chair back loudly and stood up to leave without paying. Instead of being outraged, my waiter appeared from nowhere and hurried over with the bill, minus the soup, as if he had been wondering when I would finally catch on. As I reached the door, a young waiter rushed up and said softly in excellent English that white borscht was an Easter soup, not available in the winter. "Why didn't my waiter just tell me?" I asked. He gave what I was starting to recognize as an Eastern European shrug. Later, I realized I should have known that the restaurant used the same tourist menu year-round, with all the seasonal specialties listed whether they were available or not.

I never did find white borscht on that trip. The closest I came was a supermarket packet of powdered *zurek* (a close relative), which turned into lumpy papier-mâché paste when I tried to make it with hot water from the hotel room tap. I did take away two lessons, though: never travel without doing your research, and never, ever visit Auschwitz alone in February.

What follows, miraculously, is a recipe I found for that Polish coffee shop white borscht.

Christine's White Borscht

(from Arthur Schwartz's *Soup Suppers*)

4 cups water

2 pounds sauerkraut (not canned), not drained

2 or 3 chicken legs

3 small bay leaves

4 medium celery ribs

2 medium carrots

2 large leeks, white part only

2 teaspoons whole allspice

2 quarts water

Coarse sea salt and freshly ground pepper

2 teaspoons dried marjoram

4 teaspoons cornstarch

1 cup heavy cream

½ to ¾ pound kielbasa, sliced, at room temperature

For the garnish:

6 medium boiled potatoes

3 hard-cooked eggs, cut into halves

1. In a 2- to 3-quart saucepan, bring the 4 cups water to a boil. Add the sauerkraut and simmer, partially covered, for about 30 minutes.

2. Strain the liquid while it is still hot and reserve. There should be about 5 cups. (The sauerkraut can be discarded; its flavor is much diminished.)

3. While preparing the sauerkraut stock, make the chicken broth: In a 3- to 5-quart saucepan, combine the chicken, bay leaves, celery, carrots, leeks, allspice, and 2 quarts of fresh cold water. Bring to a brisk simmer over high heat, reduce heat, partially cover, and let simmer steadily for 1½ hours.

4. Strain the chicken broth and reserve. There should be about 4 cups; if not, add a little water.

5. In a 4- to 6-quart pot, combine the 4 cups chicken broth with 4 cups of the sauerkraut stock. Season to taste with salt and pepper. Cover and bring to a boil. Add the marjoram.

6. In a small cup or bowl, mix the cornstarch with the remaining cup of sauerkraut stock. Whisk into the briskly boiling soup and cook for 1 minute, stirring slowly. This will not perceptibly thicken the soup, but it will bind it.

7. Turn off the heat and stir in the heavy cream.

8. To serve, place several rounds of kielbasa, a boiled potato, and half an egg into each wide, deep bowl. Ladle on the hot soup.

Serves: 6

Advance preparation: Can be kept refrigerated for up to a week (don't worry if it separates); it freezes perfectly. Reheat to a simmer before serving.

is for

Lobster Roll

Everything has its price, as my divorce attorney was fond of telling me, so I was willing to endure the protracted financial blockade necessary to extricate myself from my second marriage. It felt like being starved out of the ghetto at Lodz. Although deep in debt, I badly needed a break from the citywide cabin fever that seizes Manhattan in August, when the only people left on the streets skulk like wallflowers who haven't been asked to dance. I had chosen a guesthouse in Kennebunk, Maine, based on glowing online reviews, but my spirits plunged as I turned off a leafy lane into the asphalt parking lot of a squat beige brick building, unmistakably a former Catholic school. Any hope that I had mistaken the address was immediately quashed by a maroon sign on the facade proclaiming FRANCISCAN GUEST HOUSE in towering block capitals. Bearing witness to its past as a dorm in a Lithuanian boys' boarding school, my room was decorated in a style that can only be called Mid-Century Misery. Paneled in a sickly yellowish brown, its ceiling bloomed with water stains, and its worn brown indoor–outdoor carpeting was suspiciously damp to the touch. Furnishings consisted of a rickety wooden desk and a bed covered with a scratchy polyester coverlet. Throwing open the windows and switching on the juddering ancient air-conditioner did nothing to dispel the almost unbreathable miasma of mildew that seemed to ooze from the walls and the floor. I descended to the front desk, where I was informed that a recent leak was responsible and that all other rooms were occupied.

Unable to afford other accommodations and unwilling to turn around and drive home, I returned to my room. Changing into my bathing suit, I could feel the mildew seep into the pores of my exposed skin. I drove to Mother's Beach, scoured myself in the ocean, and fell asleep in the sun despite the shrieks of happy children. I woke up slightly sunburned and extremely hungry. One of the few treats I had planned was dinner that evening at Mabel's Lobster Claw, said to be the elder President Bush's favorite restaurant, but it was only five p.m. and my reservation was not for hours. Spending time in my room was out of the question, so I drove across the river into Kennebunkport to get the lay of the land. Less than a mile along a coast road, I saw the sign for Mabel's. I'd had no idea where it was, so it seemed like an omen. Why go back to that depressing room to shower and kill time when it was right in front of me? The place looked casual enough, with outdoor seating—now empty—under a bright blue awning. I parked the car along the edge of the dunes, tied my black beach sarong over my bathing suit, knotted my shirt, and tucked my damp hair under a rather elegant straw hat. Brushing the sand off my feet and donning a pair of simple black sandals, I thought I looked quite presentable.

I knew the instant I walked through the door that I had made a mistake. Although the hostess treated me kindly, even charmingly, I felt like I had when I was six and came down to breakfast in a hotel in my pajamas. No one in Kennebunkport would spontaneously walk into a restaurant off the beach. The male customers were dressed in crisp, nautical whites and blues, the ladies in print dresses accessorized with oversized summer costume jewelry. They were too well-bred to whisper about me, but their looks of indulgence were almost worse. The waitresses were friendly, almost maternal, but my discomfort increased when I opened the menu. The prices were steep even by Manhattan standards. All of the "famous" lobster dishes cost more than fifty dollars, so I ordered what I could afford, a steamed chick, 1⅛ pounds, which came with a cup of clam chowder, a house salad, and a baked potato. To paraphrase Woody Allen, the food was terrible—and such small portions! Most depressing of all, the lobster was rubbery, its scrawny tail so chewy I couldn't cut it with my butter knife. After finishing my roll and the skin of my baked potato, I was still hungry, but the waitresses were so nice that I lied when they asked if I had enjoyed my meal. I turned down the proffered blueberry pie and left. So this was the favorite restaurant of the former president of the United States? He could eat anywhere in the world, and he preferred Mabel's? As I fell asleep in my moldy bedroom, the steaming streets of Manhattan didn't look so bad after all.

Despite glorious weather, the morning was no better. The promised homemade Lithuanian pastries and cheeses nowhere in evidence, the breakfast buffet was a pallid spread of weak coffee and quartered oranges, Cheerios, and toast. I had yet to adopt the cheerful make-do attitude of the professionally frugal guests who surrounded me. Once again, I got up from the table hungry. Although the guesthouse was on the wrong side of the tracks, it was within walking distance of town. As I crossed the bridge and saw the parade of blinding white shorts and white teeth, golden hair and tasteful gold jewelry, red pedicured toes and waxed, tanned limbs, I felt a poignant stab of nostalgia for Martha's Vineyard. My husband and I had spent the last ten summers on the Vineyard, where the rich dressed like the islanders and there was no way to tell who owned a thirty-four-foot sloop and who scraped the hull, where everyone went barefoot and everyone's car was covered with the same ubiquitous island dust. Like a punch in the midriff, it hit me that I had been doubly exiled from my former life, by poverty and by impending divorce. The Vineyard was my husband's territory. I missed the affluence but even more, perhaps, the modest way it was carried. I missed being half of a prosperous couple, with a big house and a crowd to cook for. I missed the way money cushioned the harsher realities. So this was the price of freedom. I saw decades of want and loneliness stretching before me.

But I also saw a long line stretching in front of a place called the Clam Shack.

Perched next to the bridge over the Kennebunk River that separates the haves from the have-nots, the jaunty little white and red building clearly had something besides looks to offer. Like any good New Yorker, when I saw a line, I joined it. By the time I arrived at the screened windows where orders were taken by preternaturally good-looking teenagers, I had observed that most people seemed to be carrying red gingham paper boats filled with picture-perfect lobster rolls. Despite the punishing price of seventeen dollars, I resolved to try one. The sign claimed that the roll contained a pound of lobster meat, and besides, I was starving. Rounding the corner, I sat down on a shady crate by the river where I could eat while watching the glittering crowd unobserved.

My judgmental musings were cut short by the first bite. Was this the best thing I ever tasted? The sandwich was a delicately balanced creation. The warm, pillowy roll, like a round hotdog bun, had been grilled in butter to form a thin layer of crunch before being spread with mayonnaise. Heaped inside and smelling only of the sea was a pile of chilled lobster meat. Drizzled with more butter, the flesh—bright red outside, snowy within—was a perfect balance of firm and tender. Inspection revealed it to be an intelligent medley of tail, claw, and knuckle meat, each contributing a different texture. When only a lemon wedge remained in the paper boat, I was completely satisfied, envying no one.

I ate every meal at the Clam Shack from then on, eventually branching out to try the other *spécialité de la shanty*: wholebelly clams. These, too, were shockingly good, a new sensation. Deep-fried and scalding, they exploded in the mouth like tender little bombs. I now understood the definition of a "poor man's feast." All right, maybe seventeen dollars for a sandwich didn't exactly qualify, but the food at the Clam Shack was so extraordinary, so pure and humble, that it managed to create an oasis of democracy in the midst of the strictly stratified local society. Twice a day I was welcomed, nourished, made to feel part of the human race again.

is for

Melon

Avalon in the 1960s was paradise for a child, wholesome in a way that seems more foreign to me now than Saigon— the Baby Parade, the Fireman's Clambake, silver dollar pancakes after church. I spent every summer with my grandparents in that southern New Jersey seaside town until, one year, I was abruptly expelled by puberty. My grandmother was like God in the Book of Genesis. She loved children in their innocence, but once they discovered free will and couldn't run around naked anymore, they got booted out of Eden in a hurry. Still, Eden it was. Even at four or five I had seen enough darkness to appreciate my grandparents' unselfconscious goodness. Their curtains were always open. Unlike my parents, who were more likely to receive a visit from a bill collector or a bail bondsman than a friend, they had no secrets. The glorious relief of that was as tangible a pleasure to me as the summer sunshine.

My grandmother's happiness increased incrementally with the number of people in her kitchen, and nothing guaranteed the cheerfulness of her sometimes volatile nature like cooking for the neighbors and relatives who streamed through from Memorial Day to Labor Day. The daughter of Italian immigrants, she was obsessed with procuring the freshest ingredients decades before it became fashionable. Fruit and those vegetables that didn't come from my grandfather's garden came from the self-described huckster, whose dark green truck inched down our quiet street two afternoons a week. Long before we saw him, we could hear his voice calling, "Can-ta-loupe, sweet corn, can-ta-loupe." The produce beneath the truck's canvas flaps was usually fresh enough to please my grandmother, but like any Italian housewife worth her *fiore di sale*, she took pride in keeping him up to the mark. She and I would come back to the house bearing armloads of corn, paper bags full of string beans (which I detested endlessly snapping and stringing at the kitchen table) and several cantaloupes, at least one of which was left to ripen for my grandfather's arrival on Friday evening. That melon would sit on the kitchen counter like an olfactory time bomb, its ever more insistent odor counting down to readiness.

Some things never changed in Avalon, and I knew that when I returned to visit with my boyfriend ten years later, there would be a melon sitting on the counter, waiting. Early Friday evening, my grandfather drove to meet my boyfriend and me at the Philadelphia train station after finishing work at his printing company. It had always been our ritual in late August to stop at my great–uncle Nick's peach orchard in Hammonton to gather some of the late-ripening fruit the pickers had left on the trees. As the three of us walked between the rows in the early evening sun, my grandfather spotted a softball-sized peach so ripe it was nearly purple. Still agile at seventy, he climbed an aluminum ladder to pluck it from the branch. Cradling it in huge hands stained with printer's ink, he deftly twisted it in two without bruising the delicate skin and offered us each a sunset-streaked half, webbed scarlet in the center where the pit had been. The taste of that peach, unctuous and perfumed, which we ate folded over at the waist so that the juice dripped onto the dirt instead of down our shirts. . . . We filled two cardboard cartons with equally ripe specimens for the cobbler my grandmother would slide into the oven to bake during dinner. Although we placed them on the backseat as gingerly as Fabergé eggs, they burst during the trip, as they always did.

Dinner, though as delicious as I remembered, was not a success. Despite my efforts to hide it, my grandparents knew my boyfriend and I were living together and disapproved, although they did their best to be welcoming. My boyfriend, while attempting to be polite, was visibly impatient with my grandmother's stream of chatter. When I took him for a stroll through the sea mist that night down the half-mile boardwalk to the tiny skeeball arcade and shell shop, I could tell that Avalon's quiet charms were lost on him. He vetoed chocolate-dipped soft serve at the Avalon Freeze, with its neon cone sign; he wanted homemade ice cream. The next morning, when I emerged from my (separate) bedroom, I found him sitting on the sofa next to my grandmother, a stack of photo albums on the coffee table in front of them, another spread on her knees as she identified member after member of the extended family. He looked as if he had been held hostage for a week. "Help me," he mouthed, and I'm ashamed to say I rebuked her and removed the photo album from her hands as I took him off to find the *New York Times*, without which he could not function, no matter how remote his surroundings. The rest of the weekend was no better. Cinnamon buns and jelly doughnuts from the bakery were silently judged tacky, as were Philly cheesesteaks and Hoy's 5 & 10 and my grandfather's dozing and watching the Phillies on TV all day. Even the beach was a frustration to him since I knew the local breakers like the back of my hand and rode almost every wave until I scraped my chin on the sand. I am to blame, of course, for choosing someone incapable of appreciating who and what I loved. It was part of the price I agreed to pay for reinventing myself. When you cut off the past, you cut it off at the root.

Perhaps he was relieved to depart before six o'clock Monday morning to beat the traffic—I know I was—but the pre-coffee malaise, grainy eyes, and vague nausea of getting up at five a.m. are never pleasant. No matter how early the hour, though, my grandmother believed in eating breakfast. All weekend, the cubed cantaloupe had sat in its airtight Tupperware container, brought out at breakfast and dessert on Saturday and Sunday, slowly digesting in its own enzymes, until the seal was broken Monday morning, releasing an overwhelming cloud of overripeness.

My grandmother thrust the reeking container under my boyfriend's nose.

"Have some cantaloupe," she said.

He drew back and put up a protective hand. "No, thank you, Mrs. A."

"Come on now," she said, her voice taking on an edge. "Eat it up." How that expression made me cringe. I sneaked a look at his face for the grimace I knew I would find there. Part of the reason I loved him, although it made me feel horribly disloyal, was that he hated the same things about my family that I did.

"No, really," he said, raising a well-defined eyebrow at me to intercede.

Here was the battle that had been brewing all weekend. I was being asked to choose sides, and I hadn't even had coffee yet.

I looked my grandmother in the eye and said in my most menacing voice, "He . . . doesn't . . . want . . . any . . . cantaloupe."

There was an awful silence. Then she raised the container above her head and let it drop. Chunks of melon splatted and slid across the kitchen floor as she rushed past us and slammed her bedroom door.

My grandfather had been shaving in the bathroom and did not witness this scene, but she did not come out to say goodbye, and the two-hour drive back was nearly silent.

That night the telephone rang. My grandfather wanted to know what I had done to my grandmother, who had apparently been crying all day. I tried to explain that all I had done was say my boyfriend didn't want any cantaloupe, which she had tried almost literally to force him to eat.

"You apologize to her," he said.

"But he didn't want it," I argued, "and then she made a terrible scene. It was only cantaloupe, for God's sake."

"I don't care if she was wrong. She's your grandmother. You apologize."

I could count on one hand the number of times I ever heard my grandfather issue a direct order. He rarely had to. I called her and apologized.

What I learned that day was nothing so simple as respect for my elders. I already knew that there were some elders you respected (him) and some you didn't (her). What kindled in me instead was the first faint suspicion that there might be something more important than being right. And in that suspicion lay the spark of compassion. As the words of apology came out of my mouth, rote and reluctant at first, I saw developing before me, as in a Polaroid, a picture of the harsh self-centeredness of my behavior. I had not let her feed us. I had upset her. I had left her feeling useless and alone in an empty house with an empty week of shortening summer days to fill. The remorse I felt was painful but salubrious. It was right to feel bad about rejecting that melon, that last fruit of summer going ineluctably from ripeness to rot, like a girl growing up to betray her grandmother at the lift of a strange man's eyebrow.

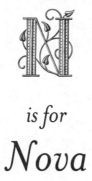

is for

Nova

Moldering somewhere in a basement or attic, if it hasn't been thrown away, is a square plywood board painted with eleven stick figures, ten of them wearing triangular hats. A wobbly banner reading CAMP ROCKHILL 1973— BUNK G-6 floats above their heads, and under their stick feet are the words 10 JAPs AND A CAP. To dispense with the political incorrectness, "JAP" stands, of course, for Jewish American Princess. I was the solitary CAP (Catholic American Princess), identifiable by the absence of a hat. The earliest of these Camp Rockhill "bunk plaques" were painted on pilfered toilet seat lids to mimic Grateful Dead album covers, which were still the desired template, but we lacked the requisite artistic talent. If the plaque has survived, odds are it is in the possession of a lifelong Rockhill camper named Carolyn, our self-appointed leader. In any other setting, Carolyn would have been a mean girl, but Rockhill was a utopia, which in this case denotes a place where mean girls were successfully encouraged to use their powers for good. Cruelty sputtered and died there like a flame deprived of oxygen.

Camp Rockhill had been a traditional summer camp for decades before Irv and Tyler Stein bought it in 1971, whereupon it became for a few brief years the embodiment of all that was best about the sixties: a heady mixture of love, freedom, experimentation, nonconformity, and a certain innocence. There is disagreement about when the sixties ended, but the era indisputably lasted well beyond the numerical decade—at least until October 1973, when the draft was abolished. I attended Rockhill in the summers of 1973 and 1974, and between those two years, I registered a subtle but unmistakable hardening of the atmosphere. At first I thought it was I who had toughened between the tender age of twelve and the more knowing one of thirteen, and perhaps I had, but there was no mistaking that Rockhill felt less like a commune and more like a camp when I returned that second July. Although the camp managed to hold on to some of its original spirit for several more years, it was eventually closed down in

1979. Rumor had it that the closing was precipitated by the counselors' being caught smoking dope with the campers; public records indicate that the cause was simple bankruptcy. But anyone who spent a summer there knew that what truly killed Rockhill was the seventies.

Rockhill's brochure promised "Health and Happiness in the Highlands" at the oxymoronic elevation of 505 feet and made do with a pool instead of a lake, but my parents had no idea of the camp's limited facilities, just as they had no idea that I would be the only non-Jewish camper. They heard the name Rockhill somewhere and they sent me there. That was their idea of research. Throwing a socially maladjusted Catholic girl into a situation where she was, by definition, the odd girl out should have been a guarantee of disaster, but for once I benefited from their impulsive style of decision-making. My bunkmates attributed the rough edges that had made me something of a pariah at school to exoticism rather than awkwardness. By the time they began to suspect the truth, Carolyn had already decided that I was her summer Pygmalion project. After making me pay with some very mild hazing that involved dipping my hand in lukewarm water while I slept the second night and smearing my face with toothpaste the following one (perfect environment or not, she was still a mean girl, the way a vampire is a vampire whether or not she drinks your blood), Carolyn began systematically reprogramming my faulty social circuits, using the same techniques she would have employed anywhere else to make my life a living hell. Where she went, the bunkmates followed, if they knew what was good for them.

What I was not prepared for was homesickness. I had spent every summer since I was three years old at my grandparents' house in Avalon, but I hadn't realized how different it was to be away from family. About a week into the eight-week session, lying in my bunk just after lights out, I was assailed by a violent spasm of longing for my bedroom and for my parents, followed by nauseating dread at the thought of spending an entire night lying in the dark among strangers. A sob escaped my throat before I could muffle my face in the pillow, and my weeping was embarrassingly audible in the silence broken only by crickets. One by one my bunkmates piled on my bed, patting my back and asking what was wrong, but their unexpected sympathy made me cry harder. Soon I was gasping and hiccoughing and began to panic because I couldn't catch my breath. The counselor on night duty had just turned on the light and asked if I wanted to go to the infirmary when the heavy thud of boots shook the porch. Even hyperventilating, I registered Rusty filling the doorframe. A lanky and taciturn Vietnam vet who was never without his shotgun, Rusty was an odd choice for camp security. No one had ever seen his eyes because he invariably wore aviator sunglasses, even at night, just as he always wore a headband around his frizzy, shoulder-length red hair and an unbuttoned denim shirt, sleeves hacked off at the shoulder. He lived somewhere in the woods, instead of in the camp buildings with everyone else, although we never pinpointed exactly where. He would simply appear—like now.

He banged the butt of the gun on the floor and everyone stopped talking mid-syllable. The only sound was the weird, gasping, hiccoughing sobs that kept coming from my throat. He turned his dark glasses on me and growled, "What's going on here?" Immediately the babble of voices started up again, trying to explain that I was homesick and couldn't stop crying. At some point my bunkmates had scrambled off the bed and formed a protective half-circle in front of me. He walked through them as if they weren't there and grasped the iron rail at the foot of my bed, lifting it over his head so that I tumbled toward the wall. I was so shocked that I stopped crying. Then he dropped the bedframe back onto the floor and walked out, telling us over his shoulder to turn off the light. I suppose it was the equivalent of slapping a hysteric across the face. In any case, it cured me, not only of the hysteria but also of the homesickness, which never troubled me again. Rusty was a good example of Rockhill's policy of radical tolerance, which took a person who might have been a serial killer in another context and made him just another member of the community.

Actually, it probably wasn't having my bed dropped on the floor that cured me of my homesickness. It was the kindness of my bunkmates, who had tried to comfort me, had stood up to Rusty for me, had even put their bodies between him and me. They had seen me weak, and instead of trying to take advantage, they had tried to help. I had never experienced anything like it.

I don't know why I was so deficient at reading social cues. Perhaps it was that I was an only child, or that I had always been a year younger than my classmates because of the public school system's dunderheaded policy of having children skip kindergarten. In elementary school, I had tried to gain some social status by becoming a bully, but I was terrible at it, and no one is more disliked than a failed bully. But now, following Carolyn's lead, my bunkmates had decided to educate me rather than ostracize me for my unacceptable behavior. When, for example, I got up in the middle of a pinochle game and wandered away because I was bored, they would say, "Come back here. You can't just leave a game like that," instead of rolling their eyes and never asking me to play again. When I corrected someone's grammar or pronunciation, Carolyn would tell me in no uncertain terms, "No one likes a know-it-all." When I made fun of Lisa for her habit of showering with her clothes on, Carolyn's more tactful sidekick Michelle would take me aside and softly tell me that Lisa had her reasons for being modest. So I started to recognize the exchange of looks that would accompany one of my many faux pas and preempt the correction by asking what I had done. Gradually, my rough edges were smoothed away. Sometimes I felt as if I were a visiting Martian mastering the baffling customs of the Earthlings, but there is nothing like living with the locals for learning a foreign language.

The Beatles provided the soundtrack for the summer, beginning with the mornings. Our usual reveille was the rooster's crow from the start of "Good Morning Good Morning," broadcast at earsplitting volume over the PA system. The first time I heard it I was on my feet, heart pounding, before I knew I was awake. Then I heard Irv's reassuring voice crooning, "Rise and shine, campers, it's a beautiful Rockhill morning!" On those Rockhill mornings that were less than beautiful, he would add, "Longs and longs," which we would throw on before brushing our teeth and stumbling to the dining hall. Only because it was breakfast would we refrain from the exasperating chant we used at other meals, complete with fork and plate-rattling hand gestures: *Food* (fists bang on table) *Waiter* (thumbs) *Waiter* (index and middle fingers) *Waiter* (pinkies), *FOOD* (fists) *Waiter* (thumbs) Waiter (index and middle)! That was one of the ways in which Rockhill was just like any other camp. Within days I learned to melt half a stick of butter into my bowl of oatmeal before stirring in several spoonfuls of sugar. Part of the fun of leaving home is picking up other people's bad habits.

The first Saturday, though, I was in for a shock. There was a hum of anticipation and no oatmeal. Instead, the center of the table was already loaded with piles of bagels, squares of cream cheese, plates of shiny tomato and sliced red onion, and platters of something orange and slightly slimy looking that everyone lunged for at once.

"It's nova!"

"No, it's not. It's lox."

"We always have nova at home."

"I don't care. Pass me that!"

"You pig! Leave me some."

Everyone forked a square or two onto her plate—where it sat looking very unappetizing and smelling vaguely fishy—until each girl collected the other ingredients she needed before assembling, with an air of practiced concentration, an open-faced sandwich to her particular specifications. I watched as they chose a specific type of bagel, spread it—or didn't—with cream cheese, and added—or didn't—tomato and onion, ignoring my questions until each of them had taken a large mouthful and smiled with satisfaction. Then they were willing to talk.

"What *is* that?" I said.

"What do you mean?"

"*That*," I said, pointing.

Completely dumfounded, their eyes followed my finger. Any doubts they'd had that I was a Martian were now confirmed.

"You've never seen *lox* before?" Carolyn demanded. When I admitted I hadn't, voices chimed in again.

"It's salmon."

"We have it every Saturday. It's a tradition."

"You know, for Shabbat. After temple."

They had me again.

"You mean like Sunday breakfast after church?" I asked.

There was a silence until someone nodded slowly. Then they resumed their argument about which was better, lox or the thing they called nova. By then, there was nothing left on the platter, so someone held out her bagel for me to try. Probably Michelle. She was the only one nice enough to do something like that. I took a bite. Improbably, it was delicious. The thin layer of orange lox fused with the tangy cream cheese, its richness offset by a dense, chewy bagel of a variety now nearly extinct. I didn't like the squish of the tomato, though, which undermined the creamy texture (and visually clashed with the pinkish orange lox). As for the raw onion, I already knew I hated it and made sure to bite around it. So I had my own formula ready for next week when I dove into the fray with the rest of them. The only choice left was whether to assemble it on a poppy or a sesame bagel.

Now I know that what was served was old-fashioned belly lox, which is not smoked but instead cured in brine. The "nova" some of them claimed to prefer was the far less salty Nova Scotia smoked salmon. But along with some *alte kackers* (I picked up a lot of Yiddish at camp), I retain a fondness for the real thing. It may have been salty, but its bracing brininess seemed an appropriate introduction to this new world.

As I was soon to discover, an even more time-honored way of learning a language than living with the locals and sampling their cuisine is having a native boyfriend. Technically, I'd had my first kiss with a camper named Stuey on the night of the first big campfire. The kiss was not the highlight of the evening—all I remember is the awkwardness of having to hunch because I was taller than he was. The full-color movie memory I retain of that night, complete with smells and sensations, is of swaying as a body with my bunkmates, arms entwined, as we sang "In My Life" and feeling the glorious warmth, after so many years of baffled yearning, of *belonging*. Stuey was not, obviously, the boyfriend. That came out of the blue one afternoon during rest period, when an emissary arrived on our porch from the boys' side with a message that one of the CITs liked me. Counselors-in-training were neither fish nor fowl, so they tended to socialize almost exclusively with each other. While they were permitted to fraternize with campers, they didn't usually want to. The male CITs were mostly waiters, as this one was. His name was Jeff, he was fifteen, and he was a dead ringer for the young Elliott Gould. Although I looked older, I was only twelve; I was new to camp and a bit awkward. Which is to say he was completely out of my league. Nevertheless, he inexplicably and openly sought me out at every opportunity. He came by and hung out on our porch during free periods (no boys in the bunks was one of the camp's few rules). He crowded onto my towel at the group swim and saved me a seat at the outdoor movie. One day he came by the bunk during rest period and asked me to come for a walk. Sitting half hidden by the enormous oak that unofficially separated the boys' camp from the girls', I had my first real kiss, the one where he looked into my eyes and buried his hands in my hair before everything around us dissolved and disappeared. So began my lifelong love affair with Jewish men, which encompassed almost every one of my serious boyfriends and both husbands. It only occurred to me later, after reading *Portnoy's Complaint*, that one explanation for

Jeff's interest in me might have been that I was the only non-Jewish girl at camp.

Our relationship caused a major stir because it contravened the natural order. My bunkmates were puzzled and more than a little jealous, but it was the female CITs who were seriously angry. There was a scarcity of age-appropriate males for them, and they were not at all pleased that a new camper had skimmed off such an attractive one. They didn't understand how he could prefer me to them, and frankly I agreed. I, too, would have chosen Sue, with her delicate aquiline nose and porcelain Madonna's face surrounded by a corona of frizzy golden hair. Or brazen, foul-mouthed Cindy in her bikini top, hipbones jutting out over her cutoff jeans. Or green-eyed, slightly zaftig Wendy, who came closest to embodying the warm and accepting spirit of Rockhill. She exhibited an easy naturalness with boys that I'd never encountered before, an assumption of equality based on shared values and background, as if they belonged to one big family. Watching her interactions with them was the first time I ever thought of boys as *human beings* rather than the "opposite sex," the enemy.

It was here, I discovered, that the great divide lay between Catholics and Jews, and I had been raised on the wrong side of it. Jewish boys and girls genuinely seemed to like and respect each other. At least for the non-religious Jews I was getting to know, sex was not disputed territory, so all relationships were not defined by it. Catholics, on the other hand, were so busy wrangling over sex—boys wanting it; girls pretending not to and either agreeing or refusing to grant it—that they had no energy left over for anything else. At Rockhill, even the accepted phrase for sexual adventures—"going out to the fields"—although purely descriptive, sounded Elysian to me. There was none of the sniggering and demeaning gossip I was used to about which girls did and which didn't. I hadn't even been aware of the atmosphere of hostility and constant wariness I lived in until I encountered an environment where it was absent, but it goes a long way toward explaining why I have always preferred Jewish men.

Not surprisingly, this basic difference in outlook between the two religions is reflected in the structure of their institutions. Catholic schools, for example, are founded on the basic principle that, having been born with Original Sin, children are bound to get into trouble if left to their own devices. When I transferred from public junior high into Nazareth Academy, it felt like going to reform school, except that I was being punished for a transgression I hadn't yet committed. Catholicism is, after all, a religion that punishes you for thought crimes (as Jesus said, thinking it is as bad as doing it). Rockhill proceeded from exactly the opposite premise. According to Irv and Tyler's philosophy, an amalgam of secular Judaism and sixties liberalism, anything you did was all right unless and until someone told you it was wrong. Camp wasn't anarchy, exactly. You had to be somewhere at every given moment of the day, it just didn't matter where. When I first arrived, I felt something was lacking and blamed it on the unconstrained schedule, but then I realized that the only thing missing was the presumption that I must be up to no good.

Toward the end of the summer, the counselors chose a line or two from a Beatles song to describe each of us and painted them on a board—what was it with those boards? I only remember two of them, mine and Michelle's. Inevitably, hers was "Michelle, our belle, we love you we love you we love you. That's all we want to say." Her name felt like more than just a neat coincidence since it was impossible not to love her; we all did. She was soft-spoken, tallish, with straight brown hair to her hips; thin but full-breasted, with big brown doe eyes, a shy smile, and a gawky long-limbed grace that suddenly coalesced one day during Color War, when we saw her run. She had an older sister named Sherry, a CIT, who was as brash and self-assured as Michelle was self-effacing. Their faces were similar, but Sherry was shorter and sturdier. It had been a long race, and everyone but Michelle had dropped out of sight. Cheering spectators lined the course, marveling in disbelief at the astonishing effortlessness of her running. She was leaping, hardly touching the ground. In my memory she is barefoot, and that may be true. As she approached the finish line, the cheers rose to a roar—and then I spied Sherry, a short-legged engine huffing up from behind, sneakers kicking up a cloud of red dust, sweat streaming off her face, teeth gritted with effort. The only other time I have ever seen a face so intent on winning has been on television, in slow motion, on the face of a champion athlete. Sherry was gaining on Michelle, who glanced back over her shoulder seeming puzzled that anyone could get so worked up over a race. I don't know whether she slowed down purposely, but she didn't speed up, and Sherry came from behind and burst across the finish line half a step ahead of her, doubled over, her face a deep crimson. Michelle, who had not even broken a sweat, went over and hugged her with a serene smile.

Sherry always seemed to be in a hurry to pack as much into her life as she could. When she was killed in a car crash a year later, I remember wondering whether it was a good thing she did or if that sense of impatience contributed in some way to her death. Now I realize that most of us are incautious and even reckless at sixteen, and we don't pay for it with our lives.

The other lyrics I remember from the boards are, of course, those that pertained to me. Group opinion regarding myself was nothing like so unanimously warm, and the lines chosen from "Across the Universe" suggested that it would be folly to try to contain the words that spilled endlessly from my mouth. I remember asking Gerri, our counselor, whether that was a good or bad thing. She gave me a long, appraising look and said nothing. It's obvious the counselors were trying to find a polite way of telling me that I was what my grandmother called a chatterbox. I only shut up during those eight weeks when I was sleeping, because it was the first time I had ever met people who were willing to listen to me. Clearly my education in responding to social cues was not yet complete. Yet a seed was planted in that moment that you could have a flaw, many flaws, and be loved in spite of them—that they were part of the package of who you were, not (as I had been raised to believe) grounds for the death penalty.

When I went back to school in the fall—Jeff's heavy gold signet ring on a thin chain bouncing off my collarbone like a talisman to remind me that it wasn't all a dream—I had the peculiar experience of not being recognized by many of my classmates. I hadn't changed physically at all—I hadn't lost weight or altered my hair. The transformation was completely internal: I wasn't "that girl" anymore, the pariah everyone shunned and feared being associated with. My old nemesis made fun of the ring around my neck, but I could tell it was out of envy—not of the ring itself, which she probably did think looked a little silly, but of the power shift it represented. Her poison couldn't touch me anymore. Not surprisingly, my relationship with Jeff did not survive in the atmosphere of the real world. The difference in age and maturity was too great, and after a few months he gently told me it wasn't going to work. Even though I was devastated, the immunity held.

Once I had a teenage son of my own, I was tempted to find out what became of that lovely man-boy. Thinking back on him gave me the vertiginous lurch of pentimento—the overlay of one reality with another. How could he be at once older and more experienced than I and yet younger than my own child? This mind-bending paradox can never be resolved within the limitations of chronological time. When I located him on the Internet, I experienced viscerally the truth of Isak Dinesen's admonition: "The Earth was made round so that we would not see too far down the road." In 1998, the year my son was born, his first-born son died of leukemia in his arms. Could he have taken any joy in his life if he had known his beautiful boy would die before reaching his third birthday? Could I have taken any joy in him if I had known what would befall him twenty-five years later? The next time I am champing at the bit to know what will happen next, I will try to remember what a gift it is that the future lies hidden beyond the curve.

is for

Omul

A cheerful troop of Russian day-trippers already stands jostling and laughing on the platform at Port Baikal when our sedate little tour group arrives. We all pile onboard the *Matanya*, the modern commuter train that traces the southern tip of Lake Baikal along Siberia's old Circum-Baikal Railway. The train buffs in our group try resuming their quiet discussion of its engineering marvels, but they have to keep raising their voices to be heard over the soundtrack to the video loop—which will run for the next twelve hours—and the Russians, who sound on this hot Sunday in July like a bunch of kids let out of school for a field trip. The scenery is spectacular, and the train makes a couple of stops so we can photograph the famous viaducts and revetments. At Shumikha, where we cluster to admire an arched Italian stone wall, I notice several Russians taking long pulls from a passed bottle and suddenly apprehend the reason for their unnaturally high spirits. Not long after, we stop for lunch at Polovinny, the railway's halfway point.

Although identified as a railway settlement, Polovinny from the platform appears to be deserted, its few tumbledown buildings sinking back into the earth. Loitering behind the others as they file down the trail to lunch, I spy a man in a cap pushing an ancient high-wheeled black pram through a field of waist-high grass to the door of an unpainted house. Who is he? Where did he come from? It is an image from a dream. The unprepossessing little trail ends, surprisingly, in an idyllic river valley, protected by low hills and larch trees that filter the light to warm greenish gold. The valley is strewn, however, with upturned rowboats, dilapidated sheds, and ramshackle outbuildings, giving the impression that when one is about to fall down, a rickety new one is built onto its side. Dotted here and there are a few well-maintained houses, shaggy brown cedar like the other structures but brightened with turquoise or green shutters. Clinging to its patch of earth like a mussel to a rock, Polovinny remains a settlement after a hundred years, seeming to defy the law of nature that says we must either grow or die.

Lunch is served from the one unequivocally cheerful building in the valley, a blue and green peacock of a shack on the bend of the river. Bedecked with petunias, with a bright red bench running along one side, it is an oasis of color in a desert of timber. A few rough tables have been tented with red oilcloth, whose lurid glow is tempered by the sunlight filtering through a stand of white birch at the far corner. I am the last to arrive, and our group squeezes together to make room on the bench. The massive proprietress puts before me a dish of Siberian meat-filled dumplings, known as *pelmeni*. The main course is soup, which everyone else is already eating. There is a line for seconds. The man at the head holds out his bowl, and she uses an enamel cup to ladle it to the very brim, which seems to be expected. As he turns, a smile transfigures his weather-beaten face, but he becomes instantly grave as he negotiates the return journey to his seat, cradling the bowl in his huge, workingman's hands and freezing after each step so as not to spill a drop. His reverent concentration is so naked that I feel embarrassed watching him: these are the actions of someone who has known hunger.

The soup is called *solyanka*, which I have come to think of as Siberian borscht. It is a sort of pickle soup containing bits of beef, cabbage, salted mushrooms, tomatoes, and in this case olives, sprinkled with dill and served with *smetana*, soured heavy cream. It is spectacular. Also on the table are slices of brown bread and bottles of homemade vodka flavored with cedar. The Russians begin to sing, swaying shoulder to shoulder on the benches. Maybe it is the size of the soup pot, or of their appetites for food and drink, or their determination to wring the most out of the short, hot summer day, but I feel dwarfed beside them, as if they are giants from another age and my hungers are puny next to theirs. I soon leave to wander down to the lake. The angle of the sun changes before I hear them crashing down the trail, still singing, laughing and weaving with their arms around each other.

The bay at Cape Polovinny is always described in the travel literature as warm, but warm compared to what? Zero degrees Kelvin, the temperature at which all motion stops? And this is not just any Siberian lake, it is Lake Baikal, the deepest lake in the world and the largest (by volume if not square footage). Whooping to rally their courage, the Russians take a running leap and belly flop off a makeshift pier into the frigid water. Our Siberian tour guide, well-padded as a Nerpa seal in her black one-piece, walks over as she towels off.

"Dip your head in," she says, smiling and patting my cheek with icy fingers. "It will make you young—take five years off."

"Off my life, you mean," I reply. This trip is for my

fiftieth birthday, which I deem old enough to make me a heart attack risk.

The legend is that immersing your hands in Baikal will add one year to your lifespan, your feet two years, your head five, and your entire body twenty-five—unless it kills you instantly. I opt for two years and dip an exploratory toe into the gelid water. Holy crap! My arch cramps so violently that I barely manage to stagger back up the beach to a fallen log, where I massage my poor foot back to life.

On the platform at Slyudyanka, where the train turns around, a row of middle-aged women are selling smoked *omul*, a whitefish of the salmon family found only in Lake Baikal. *Omul* is a great favorite of the Siberians, who eat it cold-smoked and hot-smoked (as these are), salted, raw, and even "with odor," a state achieved by leaving the fish in hot sunlight for about fifteen minutes. The slightly smelly fish is then eaten raw, complete with scales and organs. There is an old joke that a man from the eastern shore goes to a fishmonger and asks, "Is this fish fresh?" Indignant, the fish seller replies, "Of course! It just came in this morning." To which the man responds, "Then I'll go someplace else." I had seen ranks of *omul* smoking unattended that morning on a blackened brazier in Listvyanka, the village on the lake where we had spent the night.

The American group leader and I quickly decide we'd much rather have *omul* than the boxed dinner offered for the return train ride, so for ten rubles, about thirty-five cents each, we buy two fish. The woman wraps them in newspaper. It is still early and hasn't been long since the heavy lunch, but soon after we sit down in the train, the smell—which our fellow group members have been teasing us about—starts to make us hungry. Happily, all of the seats are arranged around tables. We each unwrap a fish, the newspaper making a perfect placemat. My concern about a lack of utensils turns out to be unfounded. After splitting the fish with my thumbs and opening it on the table like a book, the spine lifts clean off the flesh, leaving moist, perfect chunks from which the skin peels like gold foil. Those who came by to scoff stayed to eat. In the background, however, the infernal tourist video resumed its ear-splitting blare. To the accompaniment of the same orange wildflower blooming over and over by the shore of the blue lake, the introductory Muzak gave way first to blessedly incomprehensible Russian, then to English: . . . *years old, Lake Baikal is the most ancient lake in the world. It is also the deepest, at 1,637 meters below sea level. Lake Baikal is the repository of one-fifth of the world's fresh—* From behind us comes a crash, a burst of wild laughter, the sounds of clinking glass. The Russians have been drinking for seven or eight hours straight now. Their raucous din combined with the music blasting from the speakers could be the soundtrack from the ball in Roger Corman's *Masque of the Red Death*. Finally, out of self-protection, I fall asleep.

When I wake up to use the bathroom, there is an eerie silence (or perhaps it is the silence that wakes me?). At some point the tape loop has been turned off. I turn around to see that the entire car has been felled—as if a bomb exploded. Everyone is passed out, slumped forward on the tables among empty vodka bottles and food wrappers, flopped sideways into the aisles, on their backs with arms outflung. The only sound is bottles rolling the length of the car, up and down, clinking into each other and changing course, until an announcement is made that the train is approaching Station Baikal and the dead begin groaning and stirring back to life.

is for

Passion Fruit

It says a lot about the girl I was at twenty-one that I married
the first man I met after stepping off the A train. I arrived
in Brooklyn on an early September afternoon carrying just
one unwieldy suitcase and a plastic garment bag sheathing a
gray polyester dress with a patent leather "self-belt." The
only semi-respectable dress in my mother's closet, it was
intended for job interviews, which I prayed would be successful because I had enough money to last about three
weeks. After a tearful phone call from Florida the previous
week, my high school boyfriend had kindly offered me the
sofa bed in his living room until I found a place of my own.
Sam didn't tell me that the living room was separated by

uncurtained French doors from the bedroom of the roommate he had found through an ad in the *Village Voice*, so it
was really the roommate who was being kind.

When I first met that roommate, sitting on the edge of
the sofa bed, I felt a flood of relief so powerful it was like
the adrenaline rush you get when you barely avoid side-
swiping another car. With one glance, I took in his
Wallabees, his curly hair raked into submission, his bitten
fingernails, the stretched-out crew neck of his green wool
sweater, and, clearly visible from the living room, his
lumpy single bed covered with a thin brown spread. The
clincher was the miniature beer stein filled with pencils
topping his scarred wooden bureau. In a split-second I
perceived, with that instinct that pairs people up as unerr-
ingly as chromosomes, that here was a man who had
self-control in such abundance that he would have some
left over for me. He was the solution to my deepest fear,
never articulated even to myself: that if I were permitted
to run wild, I would put myself in danger one too many
times and end up dead in a hotel room, like the heroine in
Looking for Mr. Goodbar. I was tempted to throw my arms
around him before I even learned his name.

From that moment on, winning Nathan over, gaining
entry into his chaste and boyish world, seemed a matter of
life and death to me. No damsel in distress ever engineered her own rescue more single-mindedly. Precisely

because of the qualities I coveted in him, it proved much more difficult than I anticipated. He was not used to flirting, so the obvious ploys failed miserably. During a Preston Sturges double feature at the old Regency Theater, I let my favorite boatneck sweater slip down off the shoulder nearest him, and he gingerly picked it up, as if it were a small rodent, and replaced it in its proper spot. I retreated, realizing that proximity was not working in my favor, and found a roommate in Manhattan.

In the end, the simplest strategies are best. Nathan was working as a lifeguard while studying for the LSATs, but no matter how disciplined he was, he still had to eat. In early October I began cooking dinner for him and Sam every Tuesday. They were hardly more than boys, after all, and were trying to survive on next to nothing. At the Strand, the cavernous used bookstore in the Village, I was astonished to find a small red, white, and green–striped cookbook that contained almost all of my grandmother's recipes. It was like stumbling on a family album. It had never occurred to me that these recipes were written down anywhere—my grandmother never measured anything—or that they were made the same way by anyone else. Until I went to college I hadn't even realized they were Italian food. What we ate was just food. But here were the dishes I had eaten all my life, collected in an abridged translation of Ada Boni's famous Talisman cookbook. The publication had been sponsored by the Ronzoni company, whose products were embarrassingly plastered all over its pages, but I found it reassuring to be able to find recipes almost identical to my grandmother's for spaghetti and clams, *braciole*, *baccalà* with green olives, and eggplant parmigiana. After a month or so, I decided to experiment with some dishes from the battered first volume of *Mastering the Art of French Cooking* I had also picked up at the Strand. In mid-November, over a winy boeuf en daube, Nathan announced that the following week would be the last that he could come to dinner. Starting after Thanksgiving, he said, he would be devoting himself completely to studying for the LSATs. I felt stricken. I knew enough about him to realize that once he disappeared into a new and even more stringent routine, I would never see him again. Or rather that when I did, it would be like seeing a stranger. It was next week or never.

I met Sam a few days later to give him a set of keys and instructed him to arrive a little early the following week with Nathan. I didn't share with him that I'd decided to orchestrate my entrance like a heroine of those romantic comedies I'd been overdosing on at the Regency. That Tuesday, wearing an ivory felt hat with black trim, a long string of pearls, a box-pleated skirt falling just below the knee, and pale gray T-strap shoes, I burst breathlessly into the apartment, my arms full of thirty dollars' worth of flowers that I couldn't afford.

Sam, not quite immune to my charms, exclaimed, "Oh, you look like the young Barbara Stanwyck."

"I was trying for Audrey Hepburn," I said ruefully.

"What?" said Nathan, rubbing his eyes.

So I engineered another strategic retreat, dredging up my long-dead desire to be a lawyer, and asked Nathan if we could study for the LSATs together. OK, I thought, perhaps the way to this man's heart is not through his stomach but through his brain. When we finally did get together, soon after, it seemed so natural that I can't remember how it happened.

Surprisingly, Nathan brought me home to meet his parents over the holidays, not that they celebrated the holidays. We'd been going out for less than a month. I quickly realized from random comments made by his mother and twin siblings that I was his first real girlfriend. At dinner, his mother grilled me on politics and feminism under a flame-red Danish lighting fixture while his father tried unsuccessfully to deflect her with mild witticisms. I'd known Nathan long enough to be sufficiently familiar with the party line to pass muster, but by the end of the meal I felt utterly depleted. I escaped to my room on the third floor to recuperate in a hot bath. Almost immediately, there was a knock on the bathroom door.

"It's me," she said. "I've got that book on suffrage in Victorian England I mentioned."

"I'm in the tub," I sang out, trying to sound far away.

"I thought you might like to take a look at it," she persisted.

"I'll get it when I come out," I replied in a tone I hoped was both sprightly and firm.

"No, no," she said, "I'll hand it to you." And she opened the door and walked in.

There was only one tiny washcloth within reach, and I couldn't figure out which part of me to cover with it— left breast? Right? Pubic hair? I kept switching from one to the other, thus giving her a look at everything, while she very coolly checked me over. Then she laid the book on the mat and walked out.

My former mother-in-law's breathtaking intrusiveness goes a long way toward explaining the defining quality of my former husband, a profound emotional and physical obliviousness. He wasn't an inconsiderate person, but everyone who knew him learned from painful experience that it was necessary to perform a grown-up version of baby-proofing before he came over, moving fragile vases from end tables and putting away the crystal. Sometimes he reminded me of that cartoon character from the sixties, Tobor the 8th-Man, whose enormous feet crushed every object in his path. He was also completely deaf to hints and subtleties of all kinds. It was as if he had gone deep underground as a child to escape his mother and had never reemerged. The only way to keep her from ferreting out his inner life was to make it inaccessible even to himself.

Of course, it was precisely this flaw that made me comfortable. I chose him as much for what he was blind to as for what he saw in me. It gave me a kind of privacy. At the same time, having appointed him the jailer of everything I feared in my own nature, I was bound to rebel against him eventually.

Almost exactly ten years after that Brooklyn afternoon, I found myself standing in a Manhattan publishing office handing a massive three-hole punch to another editorial assistant and asking her to hit me over the head with it so I could go home early. When she realized I wasn't joking, she confided her worries about my mental state to her boss, who spoke to mine, and some vacation time was arranged. My mini-breakdown had only partly to do with keeping afloat an underqualified woman who compensated for Olympian procrastination with pyrotechnically face-saving strokes of brilliance. The other part was that I was miserable at home.

Nathan had a judicial clerkship in Hartford, so we lived in Fairfield, Connecticut, one hour from his job and two hours from mine. I hated our first-floor apartment in a little house off the Black Rock Turnpike—beige aluminum siding outside, beige walls and carpeting inside. I was exhausted from commuting on Metro-North six days a week and working at home on the seventh. Most of all, I deeply resented him for having taken a position three years earlier at a law firm in Boston, his hometown, when he had been offered an equally good one in New York. I'd had the perfect publishing job and should have stood my ground, but I followed him, and in order to restart my publishing career I'd had to enter one rung lower than where I left off. It is shameful to realize I was so incapable of living on my own that I opted to torpedo my own career rather than take a stand that didn't even harm someone else.

The moment I heard I had a week's vacation, I was on the phone to my mother, a travel agent. Despite my being extraordinarily badly paid for my labors, she was able to book me on a "fam" trip to Margarita Island, the "Pearl of the Caribbean," off the coast of Venezuela. Eight days and seven nights at the new Hilton resort on the beach, airfare and all expenses paid, for two. "Fam" is short for familiarization, and twenty-five years ago it was one of the great boondoggles of the travel industry. All I had to do was pretend to be a travel agent and I could go for next to nothing—room, board, tours, etc.—in exchange for recommending the facility to "my" clients when I got home.

Or not. There were no strings attached. My husband said he couldn't take off work at such short notice, so I invited my friend Nancy.

Margarita Island. When I told one of the other assistants where I was going, he asked incredulously, "Are you joking? Is that next to Piña Colada Island?" Not quite, but it was paradise. It wasn't called the Pearl of the Caribbean for nothing. Unfortunately, every paradise has its serpent, and ours was a tour guide named Wilhelm, a good-looking German with chilly gray-green eyes. I could feel them on me in the hotel lobby, in the breakfast room, in the tour bus as he explained why the tree trunks along the side of the road were painted white. When I emerged from the cathedral at La Asunción, disoriented by the sudden glare, our gazes finally collided, mine skittering off like a pool ball. As I stepped into the bus later that morning, he grabbed my upper arm and pulled me back down to the ground. His lips almost to my ear, he hissed, "You pretend to be a good girl, but I know what you really are." Then he let go of my arm and smiled. I climbed onto the bus, too shaken to be angry. Nancy asked me what was wrong, but I just shook my head. I knew he was right. Being a good girl was only a charade. Staring out the window, I wondered if the powerful protection that marriage to Nathan had conferred on me was beginning to wear off, like a vaccine that loses its efficacy.

After a few lazy days on the beach, our group went snorkeling off El Farallón, a massive white rock completely colonized by masses of wheeling, shrieking birds. It was hard to tell if El Farallón was naturally white or if the years' accumulation of guano had entirely cloaked it. The underwater sightseeing was drab (the water was rough, and poor Nancy was so seasick she stayed in the boat), but one of the young snorkeling guides managed to communicate by gestures that it was possible to climb onto the island if you swam around the back. He took my mask and snorkel and threw them into the boat. It was difficult to swim against the current wearing the unfamiliar flippers, but it was exciting to approach a wholly avian universe, its inhabitants now squawking and flapping even more riotously because humans were approaching. Watching them plunging and swooping and jostling each other for prime real estate reminded me of the Times Square subway station during rush hour. Exhilarated, I felt my face stretch into a smile as I dove under the water. Coming up for breath with my eyes still closed, I was shocked by the feel of something slippery on my mouth. I opened my eyes to find the guide's face inches from mine. He had kissed me—I could smell his unbrushed teeth, see the freckles where the zinc oxide had rubbed off his nose. He put his hands on my shoulders, and my pounding heart communicated to me quicker than my thoughts how helpless I was, treading water in my awkward fins, screened from the others by the huge, noisy rock. I pushed him away, yanked off the fins, and swam as fast as I could to the boat. He didn't follow me.

Once I heaved myself over the side, breathless and wiping my face with a towel, I whispered to Nancy what had happened. Back on shore, we were still discussing whether to complain to the tour company when the other guide came over. Clearly the brother of the offender, he explained haltingly in English that Marco, whom I could see squirming with embarrassment and fear a little way off, was horribly sorry. It was a big misunderstanding, he said. Marco had thought I wanted him to. Even as I protested huffily that I was married, it occurred to me that I might have unconsciously given off some of the old signals the German tour guide had picked up on, or that perhaps the misunderstanding had been a cultural one. In any case, I could tell they were sincere, and I realized he would almost certainly lose his job if I said he accosted me. Jobs were in short supply on this island. It didn't seem fair to salve my ruffled feelings at the expense of ruining his life. I said it was okay. As we left, I turned to look back at the ocean. Marco was standing on the beach, one arm raised in a curiously solemn, almost archaic gesture of farewell.

The next day, Nancy and I took a badly needed break from organized activities and rented a car to explore the Macanao peninsula, the arid, uninhabited half of the island. The east side, where we were staying, had nearly all of the population—and the rainfall. The west, which we were driving through, was desert. After miles of nothing, we saw a man leaning on a truck parked on the side of the road. Propped on the ground against two tall aluminum cylinders was a hand-lettered sign: BATIDO DE PARCHITA. We immediately pulled over, having recognized the word *parchita* from breakfast—passion fruit. We had become addicted to passion fruit juice and now drank it from the hotel dispensers every morning. The cylinders looked cool, beaded with condensation. We were so thirsty, we flew in the face of every tenet of travel safety—don't eat any fruit you haven't peeled yourself, avoid foreign ice— and asked for two glasses. The liquid pouring from his ladle had the color and consistency of apricot nectar but it emanated an explosive perfume. Nancy and I toasted and each took a long swallow. The juice looked like nectar, and nectar it was. This must have been what the gods drank on Mount Olympus, I thought. Simultaneously tart and sweet, it produced a pleasurable shock to the palate while soothing it with a cool and satiny texture. It some-how embodied the essence of the tropics, and standing there by the roadside I felt one of the sharp jolts of free-dom that are the true reason I travel. The watery simulation we had thought so delicious at the Hilton breakfast buffet tasted like Kool-Aid by comparison.

Having washed the dust from our mouths, we turned off the road and bumped down a steep, rutted track to a beach marked on the map. Leaving our shoes, we set off, the ocean on one side and a towering cliff on the other. The beach was empty, and it was an almost physical relief to be away from the others on the tour, professional travel agents who peppered me with questions I couldn't answer about the industry in Florida. I was especially happy to get a respite from the continual, unblinking scrutiny of the guide, whom I had come to regard with an almost superstitious dread. Nancy and I walked in comfortable silence for some time before noticing that we had been joined by a scruffy dog. He trotted behind at a respectful distance, wagging his tail whenever we turned to look at him. After a while he began bounding back and forth between us and the ocean, running ahead, pausing, and racing back to walk first next to one of us and then the other, so as not to offend. In areas where people have trouble getting enough to eat, dogs are generally not welcome, and this one seemed grateful for some friendly company.

Far out to sea, an enormous bird hovered on a thermal, barely moving its wings. From its deeply forked tail, Nancy recognized it as a frigate bird, and as it rode down the currents of air toward us on its huge bent wings like a pterodactyl's, our awe turned to fear. From directly below, its wingspan appeared to be six or seven feet, and we were relieved when it began to climb again and disappeared over the cliff. Further down the beach, we spotted two boys crouched on the sand at the tide's edge, busy filling a pail. We approached and pointed, and they showed us their harvest of shiny black winkles. When the dog trotted over to inspect, they drove him off so ferociously that he hauled off until he was just a dark speck in the distance. One of the boys pried a winkle out of its shell with a pin and proffered it to me. He then gave one to Nancy. The tiny gray mollusk was chewy, sandy, salty—like eating the beach—but it didn't take up any space in my stomach. It was hard to imagine how many pails they would have to fill to satisfy hunger. We continued on, our canine companion reappearing when we were safely away from the boys. As we approached our shoes, he put his front paws in my sneakers, looking up at me imploringly with his doggy eyes, and cocked his head. Then he sprang playfully away before doing it all again, as if to show me what a charming fellow he was and what a good idea it would be to take him home.

The day before we left, eight of us loaded into two twin-engine planes and flew over Angel Falls. It was so cloudy that Nancy and I were happy just to have glimpsed a flash of something white and vertical, and there was some discussion between our pilot and the tour guide about whether it was too overcast to land at Auyán-tepuí, the enormous, Precambrian sandstone mesa from which Angel Falls originates. To our immense relief, the pilot decided to set down as planned at Camp Kavac, a small Pemon village at the base of the tepui. After lunch, the group set off on a hike led by a couple of Pemon guides. Hopping from rock to rock through swimming holes whose jasper bottoms tinted the water the color of strong tea, we followed a stream into a narrow gorge whose fern-dotted walls towered hundreds of feet on either side. Gradually, the water deepened until it rose to our chests and we half-swam, half-pulled ourselves along a rope until we reached a bend. We heard the thundering of the falls before we saw them and, rounding a corner, entered a cathedral-like cavern where the massive curtain of water surged over a cantilevered rock to slam into a dark pool. The air was filled with mist, the droplets illuminated by a crescent-shaped opening above. When I tried to swim toward the falls, the water pushed me away with such force that I made no progress, as if I were on an aquatic treadmill.

By the time we returned to the camp, a cluster of about a dozen beehive-shaped huts called *churuatas*, my lips were blue with cold. We each got our own hut, slung with a hammock in which to take a nap until it was time to fly out, but I was shivering. Finally giving up on trying to use my wide-brimmed straw hat as a blanket, I wandered outside. Across a stretch of savannah, the uncanny flat top of Auyán-tepuí rose through scraps of mist. In the far distance, a smaller tepui floated in a wreath of clouds, the valley below obliterated by fog. These massive rock formations with their trick of appearing suddenly weightless had inspired Arthur Conan Doyle to write *The Lost World*, about a land where dinosaurs still roamed the earth. They emanated something so ancient and self-contained that my overexposed cubicle and dinky little apartment back home receded into insignificance. As I compared the flimsiness of my life in the city with the landscape I looked on, the world seemed to open out and gain amplitude. Drops of cold rain began to hit my bare arms. I had been granted a different scale to measure with, one that I have never lost. Not once in the ensuing years have I again made the mistake of conflating my home life and workplace with the pulsing, multitudinous world.

The next day, only Nancy and I took the hotel shuttle to the local airport in Porlamar, where we would catch a connecting flight to Caracas. While she went to change money, I sat down in the cafeteria to have coffee and a candy bar. The tiny airport was just a landing strip of packed earth, and flies buzzed in and out through the open windows. I was idly watching a small boy behind the counter, one of those ragged children of indeterminate age who are always scurrying around trying to make themselves useful. The workers were teasing him and shooing him away. I couldn't understand what they were saying, but he seemed to laugh it off and refuse to go. Without warning, one of them pulled a can of insecticide from under the counter and sprayed it straight into his eyes. The boy clutched his face and cried out, falling to the floor. I stood up, wondering how to find a doctor, but before I could take a step the boy was on his feet again, and I perceived that it was not the first time this had happened. Hands covering his eyes, tears streaking his dirty cheeks, he was desperately trying to laugh and pretend it was all a joke. I sat back down, filled with a kind of sick horror.

I was also furious. I wanted to berate those men, but even if they could have understood me, it wouldn't have helped him. Where would he go if they kicked him out from behind the counter? Maybe they gave him food, or maybe this was what passed for affection, or at least connection, in his life. For that, human beings will tolerate almost anything. Elaborate plans for how I would adopt him began to run through my head. I would go home, find out how to cut through the red tape, jump through the bureaucratic hoops. I was married; I was a good candidate. I would come back and take him home with me. I would give him a good life. I felt it was my moral imperative to rescue him. It didn't occur to me until I calmed down a few hours later that it was impossible, that he might not even be an orphan, that he might not want to go back to the United States with a stranger. For years, I kept the red and yellow wrapper of my Cri-Cri bar as a talisman of something I didn't quite understand, something besides my own moral failure. I kept it because I, too, had made a devil's bargain not to be alone.

On the flight from Caracas to New York, I put on my headphones and listened to Joni Mitchell's *Blue*. Staring out the window at nothing, I was startled by something dripping onto the back of my hand. Tears—cool, silent tears that seemed to have nothing to do with me. I was as surprised as if I had woken to find myself crying in my sleep. I asked myself where they were coming from, and the answer came that I had not thought of my husband in days and that this was the first time in memory that I had felt free to think my own thoughts without running them through the filter of whether or not he would approve. I couldn't bear the idea of reentering mental captivity, but from this height I caught the first glimmer—which would take another two years to coalesce into a clear picture— that I had designed my own thralldom. Isak Dinesen once said that you can never know the truth about someone else's marriage. I would go further and say you can't even know the truth about your own, at least not until it's over. I have been married twice, and each time, the dawn of understanding augured the beginning of the end.

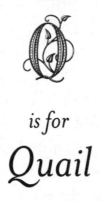

is for

Quail

When I was in my mid-twenties, in an attempt to eke out my meager editorial assistant's salary to support both me and my law-student boyfriend, I decided to try my hand at book reviewing. A friend who worked in publicity at another publishing house gave me an advance galley of a short story collection, and to my surprise and delight, several newspapers accepted the review I sent them on spec. To thank her and celebrate my success, I decided to spend half my earnings on a grown-up lunch at Arizona 206 for the two of us. In my memory, it was a blindingly sunny day, as befit a Southwestern restaurant. The walls were white adobe, smooth and undulating, as if the interior had been shaped naturally, by hands or the long action of water. Stepping down into the dining room felt like entering another country, where we sat on benches and were flirted with in a charmingly professional way by our handsome waiter. He recommended the quail, which I had never eaten before. We must have ordered other things as well, but I don't remember what they were. I do remember how shockingly tiny the birds were, how fragile their bones, and that knives and forks were useless. The only way to eat them was to pick them up and strip off the meat in a way that felt both barbaric and sensual. I remember how unabashed my friend was about it, so I felt free to be so as well. They were so crisp and lemony and aromatic with sage and thyme. And since I had to pick them up, their smell got right up into my nostrils as it would not have otherwise. When we were finished, I remember wanting more, but perhaps that is the point, as it is with caviar. Whatever else we ate, it took a long time, because we were among the last diners remaining. The light had changed by the time I asked for the bill. Pulling out the cash to pay was the best part of all. I had made that money with my own thoughts, my own words, and I had earned the right to spend it as I chose.

Perhaps it was this memory that prompted my choice of quail a decade later as the main course in the very first meal I prepared for my future in-laws. I look back now on that brisk, blue, unforgiving day at their country house north of New York City and wonder why I was cooking lunch for them in their own kitchen at all. By then I was a cookbook editor, and no doubt my future husband had been bragging about my culinary skills; my future in-laws (although they were not yet so-defined) were very serious about food. My future husband's formidable mother had been such an accomplished amateur cook in the early Julia Child era that Craig Claiborne had written her up in the *New York Times*, and their kitchen walls in the city were covered with framed menus from three-star Michelin restaurants in France. I thought I was showing off, I suppose, but I now see it in a rather darker light, as a sort of audition. From their point of view, I had not yet gotten the part.

The first course, a sort of afterthought requiring little effort, was a butternut squash soup topped with a very nineties swirl of herb butter. It was perfect for the weather and made quite a pretty presentation in little white crocks with lion's heads on the sides. It was also delicious, which was a good thing considering what came next. At that stage of my life, and even for many years afterwards, I prided myself on never making the same dish twice. So, while it was incredibly foolhardy to prepare something unfamiliar for such an occasion, there was precedent. What was even more foolish, though, was trying to reproduce a dish from a chef's cookbook on a forties-vintage electric stove. It was like trying to make pizza in an Easy-Bake Oven. I'd had the butcher butterfly eight beautiful little quail and then rubbed their skins with a special spice mixture sold by one of my cookbook authors. I heated two skillets as thoroughly as I could, seared the birds on each side for however many minutes the chef indicated, and plated them with panache. They looked and smelled delicious: so plump and golden, with their lovely crisp skin. The four of us cut into them—and found that next to the bone they were nearly raw. The spice rub had made it impossible to tell that the quail were not even approaching doneness.

What would have been an embarrassment under any circumstances was a positive disaster here: I could not have known that my future father-in-law, a Brahminish Jewish lawyer straight out of *The Sisters Rosensweig*, had a horror of undercooked poultry that amounted to a phobia. His knife and fork clattered to his plate as he announced that no one could force him to eat raw quail. I rushed to assure him that I had no intention of doing so, gathered up the offending dishes, and put the birds back in the pans for what seemed an eternity while the three of them drank wine and tried to pretend they weren't hungry. When I finally served the quail again, my future father-in-law politely nibbled a corner of one but did not attack it with the gusto the rest of us did. It hardly mattered that they were really quite good.

I thought I was safe as I brought out the cheese course, having selected three very nice specimens from Zabar's and brought them properly to room temperature. So I was taken by surprise when my future father-in-law looked me in the eye and said in a conversational tone, "You know, Dawn, with all the hundreds of cheeses in the world, it's a mystery to me why anyone would choose to serve Morbier." One of the many invaluable lessons in humility I had not yet learned was how to swallow a rebuke with good grace. I blush to say that I could hardly keep the triumph out of my voice when I replied, "I couldn't agree with you more. In fact, I only chose it because you served it to me at our last dinner together." It was an ill-advised coda to an injudicious meal and left a bitter taste unmitigated by my flawless poached pears.

is for

Rosemary

Rome at the height of the tourist season is not the place to run out of money. In this era of credit cards and ATMs, it may seem quaint even to talk of running out of money while traveling, but in the 1980s my boyfriend and I used traveler's checks, and suddenly there weren't any left. We had been running short for some time, but on the train to Roma Termini we discovered that each of us had thought the other was carrying our emergency fund, now spent. We came to this realization on a Saturday, and our plane was to leave on Monday afternoon. Even if we had been willing to cave in and ask his parents to wire money, the American Express offices were closed. It is not, however, much of an exaggeration to say that we would rather have died than admit we couldn't do it on our own. Counting up our last remaining lire and the few dollars and coins we had left in our wallets from the US, we realized we couldn't afford even the cheap hotel room we had reserved.

When we explained our situation to the clerk at the information desk, he looked at us with amused pity and handed over a list of *pensioni* near the train station. We began making phone calls. Over and over we were turned down even before we'd finished our broken Italian question, often with laughter, as if it were truly risible that anyone would expect to find a vacancy for the same night in Rome in the middle of August. I started to imagine what it would be like to sleep on a bench in the station when, near the bottom of the list, mirabile dictu, we found a room. The woman on the line said in barely intelligible English that her son would come and get us because we would have difficulty finding the place ourselves.

The Port Authority and Penn Station had taught me that it is never a good idea to stand still for too long in a place designed for passing through. Too many people make a living by preying upon the lost and confused. As we stood waiting, keeping a firm grip on our bags, I felt we were being circled by sharks. I couldn't spot them because of their protective coloration, but I knew they were there, and I sensed that the circles were getting smaller as the minutes passed. After about an hour, the bench began to look like an awful possibility. We waved off a paunchy disheveled man in a graying wifebeater, only to discover he was the proprietor's son. Too uninterested to be offended, he motioned with his cigarette for us to follow him.

Dragging our bags down grimy streets, we followed him until we arrived at a derelict building. Then we understood why she had sent him. Even as desperate as we were, we might have reconsidered staying there, but with an unexpectedly deft movement, he hustled us over the threshold and up a dirty staircase, huffing close behind with a slap of rubber slippers in a cloud of cigarette smoke. At a landing three flights up, he elbowed past and unlocked a door. We trailed reluctantly with our bags as he shuffled down a dark hall, past a lace-curtained doorway illuminated by the blue flicker of a television. At the end of the corridor, he pushed open the door to a room from a nightmare—penitentiary or psych ward—cement floor with a metal drain in the middle, two sprung cots sloppily made up with yellow-stained sheets, and a sickly reek of disinfectant that intensified rather than dissipated during the two awful days we spent there. We sat on the edge of the cots and looked at each other, but there was no time to wallow. We needed to go in search of food.

Neither of us had had quite enough to eat for the past several days, and nothing since coffee and a *cornetto* that morning, and I was about as hungry as I'd ever been or thought it was possible to be. About that I was quite wrong. Irritability, a painfully hollow stomach, and a headache are only the first stages of hunger. On a Saturday afternoon in August, whatever stores we might find would soon be closed. A few blocks away, we were lucky to come upon an *alimentaria* just locking up and begged the proprietor to let us grab a head of wilted lettuce, a hard, greenish tomato, and a plastic package of unnaturally pink ham. Back in the room, we prepared to make one of our "Starving Chef's Salads." We unpacked the soft blue plastic dish tub we had been using for this purpose since money got seriously tight. Inside it were wrapped a bottle of red vinegar and one of cheap, acrid rapeseed oil. Although rapeseed was rechristened "canola" decades later, after the invention of a de-bittering process, our bottle bore the smell of its other use: the lubrication of steam engines. It galled me that we did not have the few extra lire to buy the inexpensive olive oil that might have rendered our salads edible. This one was a particularly poor specimen and left us almost as famished as before. Even calling up the smell of rancid oil and perfumed hotel soap that permeated that soft plastic tub—what's more, recalling the hunger that made me eat what was in it anyway—makes me gag. There is a fine line between hunger and nausea, which are as close as love and hate.

The lace-curtained door was open for the first time next morning, and as we passed on our way out, the mama dragged her eyes away from the television set to berate us for eating in our room—she seemed to have a terror of vermin—and insisted that either our food-related items went or we did. I was not sorry to see the tub go, but we couldn't afford a restaurant meal, and since it was Sunday all the food stores from which we might have assembled a meager picnic were closed. We began wandering through the back streets in search of something, anything, to eat, but the spirit of commerce was not alive in Rome in August in the 1980s. Again and again, we saw the sign CHIUSO until I came to loathe the word, as I do to this day. It recalls to me blistering heat, an aching head, irritability verging on panic, and a hunger so intense it had turned to pain. Hours went by. We argued about what direction to go in and whether or not to sit and rest, but stopping would be like sinking down into a snow bank when you are freezing to death. It was late afternoon in a neighborhood even more ghostly and deserted than the others, when we caught a whiff of something, something tantalizing—roasting meat, hot fat. It struck a deep, primal chord in me, and I started to run, my boyfriend close behind. What was that delicious herb—sage? We rounded a corner, and there before us was the steamy window of a *rosticceria*, full of plump golden chickens turning slowly on spits like something out of "The Little Match Girl." It was—APERTO. Could it be? It was like a mirage in the desert, if mirages wafted out billows of delirious smells. We rushed through the door, our usual shyness swept aside by hunger. *Quanto costa questo?* The answer was a sum miraculously small even by our pauper's standards, and we bore away our prize to the lip of a dry fountain, where we tore into it with our hands. Redolent of rosemary, its skin deliciously crisp, its flesh meltingly soft, the chicken tasted like—camphor, like pine resin, no, worse—like Pear's soap. During the hours on the spit, the rosemary branches stuffing the bird's cavity had mingled with the juices and the fat and turned it into a chicken-shaped room freshener. It smelled divine and was as inedible as incense. I will never forget the despair of that first bite, which I forced myself to keep in my mouth. My brain and my stomach waged an inner battle. I fought my gag reflex. To spit it out, to admit it was inedible, would be to condemn myself to the rest of a day and an entire night of starvation. But to swallow seemed physically impossible. Thinking back, that long moment reminds me of what seems like the seminal scene of my early childhood: flanked at the kitchen table between my warring parents, holding in my mouth a bite of something I had just tasted and not liked. My mother shouting "Swallow it!" while my father, with equal volume, countered "Spit it out!" my head going helplessly back and forth, as at a tennis match, paralyzed about what to do. In the end, my mother always won. Perhaps that was why I was able to force down that first bite. My eyes filled with tears as I met my boyfriend's gaze. For both of us, self-preservation was stronger than the gag reflex. As we got closer to the cavity, the vile resinous taste grew stronger. We carried the half-eaten chicken back to the shop, which was, conveniently, *chiuso*. Did they, the only bad cooks in Italy, turn out the lights when they saw us returning? Defeated, we returned to the fountain, removed a bush's worth of rosemary from the cavity of the chicken, and finished it.

Twenty-four hours later, having eaten nothing else, we got on a plane to Boston. In the hours before we boarded, I had gone far beyond pain, irritability, and light-headedness. My metabolism had been thrown into a perverse sort of overdrive and begun burning up muscle now that the stores of fat were gone. I could actually see and feel myself getting thinner by the hour. No one who has ever starved, if even for a day or two, will ever revile safe and edible food of any kind, even if it is served on an airplane. It would be wrong to say I felt gratitude as the plastic tray was set before me. I was overwhelmed instead with a sense of the kindness of food, as if it were something sentient, with agency and my best wishes at heart.

I am glad to have been that hungry once, although it is not an experience I would willingly repeat. It cured me of the spoiled arrogance of disparaging perfectly good food that passes for refinement in some circles, as if having ever-so-rarefied tastes (sometimes masquerading as "intolerances") makes you a superior human being, a sort of princess-who-won't-eat-the-pea. But I still can't stomach rosemary.

is for

Stuffing

Whenever someone calls my Stromboli Stuffing "dressing," I have to stifle the urge to burst out laughing. Dressing is far too genteel a word for this irresistible but decidedly unrefined amalgam of white bread, Italian sausage, boiled ham, onions, garlic, butter, eggs, and mozzarella cheese. Technically, Stromboli Stuffing may be a "dressing," since it is baked outside the bird, but spiritually it is stuffing.

Stromboli Stuffing was invented by my stepfather, a man whose operative word was "more." There may be other recipes in existence like this one, but I can confidently say he never opened a cookbook in his life. So if someone else did come up with essentially the same thing, the discovery parallels the simultaneous invention of calculus by Leibniz and Newton. The dish expressed the man, who like all of us had the virtues of his vices. Excessive, irresponsible, and self-indulgent, he could also be—I must admit—a hell of a lot of fun. What's brilliant about Stromboli Stuffing is that, like my stepfather, it is pure id. No celery, no chicken stock, no herbs: nothing dutiful, healthy, or adult. While not a recipe for a successful life, it produced a great recipe for stuffing.

You can tell that Stromboli Stuffing is a real dish, an organic entity possessing integrity rather than just a cheap spinoff, because it resists all attempts to tart it up and make it into something it's not. Every time I tried to "upgrade" the ingredients—using prosciutto instead of supermarket boiled ham or fresh whole milk mozzarella instead of the eight-ounce bag of semi-skim shredded stuff—the results were disastrous. The prosciutto curled up dry at the edges; the mozzarella stretched into foot-long strings. This stuffing is what it is and wears its origins proudly.

Stromboli Stuffing debuted for me in 2001, in the Cuban mahogany–paneled dining room of a sprawling Riverside Drive apartment that my husband and I had just renovated. My stepfather had told me how to make it over the phone that afternoon.

"Dawn, this stuffing is di-vine," pronounced my

mother-in-law. "What's in it?" Conversation around the nineteenth-century dining table ceased. Scanning the expectant faces of the distinguished guests beneath the Montgolfier chandelier, I made my decision.

"You don't want to know," I replied.

Last year, it was my contribution to a friend's potluck Thanksgiving. As the guests tucked in, the expected and always gratifying murmurs of appreciation began. *What is this? What's in it?* Thinking the name would be self-explanatory, I said it was called Stromboli Stuffing.

"Oh, *Strom*boli, like the island? We were just in Stromboli!" exclaimed one couple.

"No, Strom-*bo*-li, like the sandwich," I said.

Someone at the other end of the long table half overheard and piped up. "*Strom*boli, like the volcano?"

"No, Strom-*bo*-li, like the sandwich!" I sounded like Joe Pesci in *Goodfellas*.

As I began to explain that the Stromboli sandwich is a rolled construction of dough filled with meats and cheese and baked in a pizza oven, it became clear that the name wasn't self-explanatory at all. These New Yorkers had never heard of a Stromboli sandwich. (Nor, they assured me, had the denizens of Stromboli.) The Stromboli sandwich, it turns out, is a Philadelphia specialty, a fact I had to leave Philadelphia to discover.

My stepfather is gone—along with the apartment and

everyone in it—but the stuffing remains. It's humbling to realize that, despite all our strivings, we have no idea what will survive us. My stepfather was not the sort of man to give much thought to what his legacy would be, but I imagine he would be surprised to discover it was a stuffing recipe. Lest this sound mocking, consider Brillat-Savarin's famous dictum, "The discovery of a new dish does more for human happiness than the discovery of a new star." How many of us can say we achieved that?

In the spirit of Thanksgiving, the recipe follows. Just consider your audience before you share what's in it.

Stromboli Stuffing

Obviously, the recipe did not come to me looking like this. It was refined orally over a period of years in harassed (me) but affectionate (him) Thanksgiving phone calls between New York and Florida. It took a long time to get it right, but here is the definitive 2006 version.

½ loaf Wonder Bread or similar white bread, torn into bite-sized pieces

1½ huge Vidalia onions, diced

1½ sticks unsalted butter

5 or 6 large cloves garlic, minced

1 pound sweet Italian sausage, removed from casing

½ pound spicy Italian sausage, removed from casing

2 eggs

½ pound boiled ham, torn into bite-sized pieces

8 ounces (bagged) part-skim shredded mozzarella

1. Preheat oven to 400°F. (Since you will probably be making other things on Thanksgiving, 25° in either direction will not make any difference.)
2. Put bread in bowl large enough to hold all ingredients.

3. Melt 1¼ sticks butter in extra-large skillet over medium-high heat. Sauté onions until golden.

4. Add garlic and sauté for an additional minute or two until golden.

5. Pour onions, garlic, and butter over bread.

6. Wipe out the pan. Add remaining ¼ stick butter and melt over medium-high heat. Add sweet and spicy sausage and cook through (don't overcook; the stuffing will bake for an additional 15 minutes). Set aside.

7. Add two eggs to bread mixture in bowl. Mix with hands, preferably, or wooden spoon if you must.

8. Add boiled ham and mozzarella to bread mixture. Mix.

9. Add sausage and mix. If stuffing is not recognizable as stuffing (*i.e.*, if it appears to be all meat and no bread), add a bit more torn bread. Err on the side of moistness.

10. Spoon mixture into a 9 × 13" Pyrex baking dish. (The stuffing can be made ahead to this point, covered, and refrigerated for up to 24 hours. Bring to room temperature before baking.) Bake approximately 15 minutes or until lightly browned at edges.

is for

Tarte Tatin

With surprisingly few exceptions, people who like to spend time in the kitchen fall into one of two camps: cooks or bakers. It is as rare to be equally at home with both activities as it is to be truly ambidextrous. Partly it's a matter of temperament, which is why cooks tend to be friends with other cooks and bakers with bakers. To make a gross generalization that nevertheless holds a nugget of truth: bakers are rule-followers and cooks are rebels. (Bread bakers are a spiritual breed who take their instructions from a higher authority.) More accurately, bakers get pleasure out of following instructions to achieve a precise result, whereas cooks consider it a necessary evil. But the differences go deeper. Why is it that I, as a cook rather than a baker, can calmly survey a five-page recipe for *boeuf bourguignon* but break out in a cold sweat when considering one of the same length for a *marjolaine*? Because baking is about trying to approach an ideal of perfection: you can only fail or succeed. An activity where perfection is the minimum is not my idea of fun. I get enough of that from my own superego without looking for it in the kitchen. When it comes to cooking, a dish can diverge from the recipe without necessarily being worse. It might even be better! This is true for bakers only when they become so expert at making the same thing after years of practice that they can attempt a tiny alteration. Cooks can experiment freely from the beginning. (The exception to my little rule is the French, temperamentally a nation of bakers, who speak of a dish's being "correct.")

For me, the experience of cooking is one of excitement, whereas that of baking is one of anxiety. Baking is all about the outcome; cooking is about the process. And you get to watch it happen. On the stove, for example, you can observe as mushrooms brown in a skillet or a sauce thickens in a pan. You are free to open the oven door to see how a roast is doing without being afraid it will collapse. You can taste while you are going along without fear of contracting salmonella from raw egg.

As Molly O'Neill observed in a wonderful essay, the cook's dessert—one that accommodates those resistant to following a recipe—is tarte Tatin, an upside-down tart made by caramelizing fruit in a skillet on top of the stove, covering it with pastry, and baking the whole thing in the oven. When finished, it is flipped over onto a serving plate. Any fruit that will caramelize will do, but the original apple is best. I first fell in love with tarte Tatin when working on *Simca's Cuisine* by Simone Beck, and since that time, whenever I am called upon to produce a dessert, it is what I make.

Oddly enough, I exhibited a predilection for upside-down baking from the beginning. The very first dessert I ever attempted back when I was a teenager (aside from chocolate chip cookies) was a pineapple upside-down cake, which employs the same principle of caramelized fruit on the bottom and batter on top. I chose it almost at random from *Betty Crocker's Cookbook*, and although it turned out beautifully, I don't remember baking anything again for almost a decade. My grandmother, who was my formative influence in the kitchen, had stopped baking by the time I started following her around. The only things she made in that department were *pizzelles*, thin Italian cookies that required an appliance resembling an electric waffle iron, and her justly famous peach cobbler. Cobbler, too, come to think of it, involves caramelized fruit dotted with batter. So perhaps I was programmed early to be wrong side up when it came to baking. Or, more likely, the only way I can circumvent my baking anxiety is to go about it backward: starting it on the stove with the crust on the top, where I can keep an eye on it.

My father-in-law was the most disciplined man I have ever known. Like many children of the Depression, he benefited from the GI Bill and became, by dint of education and hard work, a successful professional. (By the time I met him, he was a name partner in a midsized Manhattan law firm.) He, however, took the familiar story a step further. Born Jewish in straitened circumstances, this boy from Newton physically transformed himself into a Boston Brahmin. By the time I met him in his mid-sixties, he was upright and sinewy, with blue eyes and a shock of flossy white hair reminiscent of Robert Frost. Carrying an ancient briefcase and sporting his perpetual Turnbull & Asser bow tie and silly Protestant hat, he could have stepped from the pages of J. P. Marquand's *The Late George Apley.* In looking at his college graduation photo, it was almost impossible to detect any resemblance to the current man.

My husband and I had been married for about ten years when my father-in-law was diagnosed with terminal leukemia. Perhaps it should not have come as such a surprise when he got sick—he was nearly eighty years old—but he had so single-mindedly outfoxed the heart disease that had killed his own father that it never occurred to anyone that he would succumb to another ailment. Because of his exemplary habits, it had been a running joke among his friends since law school that he would outlive all of them. He had fiercely believed that good health, like success in all other areas of life, was simply a matter of will power and intelligence. As a trust and estates lawyer, it was his métier to outsmart the two things that everyone else avoids thinking about: death and taxes. His will was a masterpiece of complicated legal instruments, but to ensure that his heirs would never need to resort to it, he exercised like a demon for an hour a day seven days a week, kept his weight at the unnaturally low level recommended by a longevity study based on rhesus monkeys, avoided all known carcinogens—and got leukemia anyway. Now he felt betrayed. Discovering that that there was only so much uncertainty he could remove from the equation was tantamount to discovering that there is no equation at all.

My father-in-law and I had not liked each other very much during the early years. I thought he was pompous and controlling; he thought I was arrogant and unrealistic. The incompatibility of our temperaments led to mutual distrust, which gradually gave way to wariness and then to neutrality. I was surprised, then, to discover how distraught I was when he got sick. He was told he had a year, perhaps a bit longer. For the first time, I looked for opportunities to be with him. As he got sicker, I often spelled my mother-in-law at the hospital because she would not leave his bedside unless someone was there to take her place. Mostly, I just kept him company, sitting with a book in my lap as he read and dozed. It was a relief that he wasn't one for confidences.

After two rounds of chemotherapy and an unsuccessful bone marrow transplant, they sent him home. Always thin, he was now painfully so, and my mother-in-law became frantic because he had no appetite. She scoured the city for delicacies that might tempt him, but after a bite or two, he would look at her apologetically and push his plate away. One day I had an inspiration that something homemade might do the trick, so I phoned my mother-in-law and offered to make him anything in the world he wanted to eat. She was dubious, but said she'd ask him and call me back. The phone rang before I had a chance to put it down. "Tarte Tatin," she said.

I could not remember ever having made them a tarte Tatin, which was surprising given that my father-in-law was not only a fanatical apple-lover but also an inveterate Francophile. He and my mother-in-law were part of the great postwar influx of American tourists to France, but unlike most tourists, they were not people who did things halfway. When they began visiting in the fifties, you had to write a letter months in advance to secure a reservation to a Michelin three-star restaurant, and by the time I met them, they had eaten in every storied establishment from Paris to Lyon. In the 1970s, my father-in-law bought a wine vineyard in Côte Rôtie as much for an excuse to visit France twice a year as for the love of wine, hiring a tutor to teach him French while he did his morning exercises. Tarte Tatin, for him, represented a last taste both of the apples of his youth and of France itself.

On one of our early trips to Paris together, my husband had taken me to his parents' favorite cookware store, E. Dehillerin. One of my purchases was a 12 ½-inch copper tarte Tatin pan. I had never used it till that day, when I discovered why it had been on sale: it was a pan of Pantagruelian proportions. After using the required number of Granny Smiths called for in the recipe, the pan was still almost half empty. I filled it with some "eating" apples I had in the refrigerator. This, I discovered, was a mistake. Juicy apples are wonderful, but not for tarte Tatin. I tried pouring out the juice, then spooning it out, finally resorting to a turkey baster, but still the apples wouldn't caramelize. After nearly an hour, they did, but when I put the pastry on top, a gap of more than an inch remained around the circumference. It looked ridiculous, like a tiny hat on a huge head. I poked the apples under it and put it in the oven, hoping for the best. When it had finished baking and I flipped it over, juice and apples slopped over the edges of the extra-large plate. I suctioned the juice out with the turkey baster, forced the apples under the crust, and wiped the plate with a towel. It still dripped a bit, but tarte Tatin has miraculous self-healing properties: it looked good. I dropped it off at the door. Later that night, my mother-in-law phoned. He'd actually eaten an entire piece. It was more than he'd eaten in a week. To this day, I have never been as pleased with anything I've made as I was with that imperfect effort.

Given the great success of the flawed tarte Tatin, I was now inflamed with the desire to make a second one. I was determined that my father-in-law's final taste of tarte Tatin should be the Platonic ideal. This time I used my grandmother's cast iron skillet, as usual, and enlisted the help of one of my few baker friends, who was known for her buttery, flaky piecrust. The apples caramelized perfectly; she unfurled the crust off the rolling pin and crimped it expertly. When we flipped it, it glistened like topaz, the apples overlapping as perfectly as fish scales. I delivered it, but no call came. After two days, I couldn't restrain myself any longer. I phoned my mother-in-law and asked how he liked it. Although she was quick to exclaim how delicious it was, it became clear from what she left unsaid that he hadn't managed to taste it.

As I hung up, I realized that the scrupulous kindness of her tone had jarred loose a memory that had been nagging at the edge of my consciousness, like a disturbing dream that keeps rising almost to the surface throughout the day. I was fifteen years old when my father wasted away in similar circumstances, except that he was not eighty but forty-five. I had asked my father in his final days what food might tempt him, and he, too, had asked for something sweet: honey cake from the Jewish bakery up the hill. I promised to bring it when I visited the next day. My stepmother had tried to warn me that he wouldn't be able to eat it, but it didn't matter in the end. When I arrived in the morning with the string-tied white box, the hospital bed in the living room was empty. The ambulance had taken him away for the last time. Redemption can come in strange and humble guises. In its topsy-turvy way, thirty years after my first upside-down cake, tarte Tatin helped to right an old wrong.

is for

Urab Sayur

The white-gloved bellman in the lobby of the Concorde Hotel hesitated before loading our luggage onto his gleaming cart, but it was hard to blame him. Jeremy and I had traveled to Kuala Lumpur straight from a longhouse in the Borneo rainforest, and we hadn't realized how grubby our bags were until we saw them piled on the lustrous marble floor of the hotel lobby. Not that we looked much better: hygiene is challenging when one of your hosts showers alfresco with his rooster. Following the bellman's reluctant back down the corridor, we paused outside the room I would be sharing with my husband and agreed to meet in the lobby restaurant in half an hour.

I sat on the edge of the bed and unfolded the note Nathan had left at the front desk. My stomach sank at the familiar sight of his blunt, back-slanted handwriting, which made him real in a way he hadn't been for more than a week. He had missed me. He was in conference sessions all day but was looking forward to the official dinner that night, for which he had packed me some clothes, now laid out on the bedspread next to me. It's funny how self-justification works. The guilt I had been feeling vanished when I saw what he had brought for me to wear—panty hose, pumps, and a long-sleeved paisley dress he'd given me years before in one of his many bids to make me look like his mother. The neckline was too high and the torso too long, and I'd never been able to force myself to wear it, yet here it was on a bed halfway around the world reminding me of why I wanted to leave him. I hated the dress. I hated his decade-long campaign to dress me—worse, to dress me like his mother. For that matter, I hated his mother, who had asked me over dinner before I left, "So, is this Jeremy gay?"

"No," I replied, adding brazenly, "Why do you ask?"

"I just wondered," she'd said, suddenly taking a great interest in her soup.

Showered and feeling more presentable at a white-clothed table in the atrium restaurant downstairs, Jeremy and I discovered we were ravenous. Our last good meal had been at the night market in Singapore a week earlier. We had shared a plateful of flowering crab, which is a fanciful name for a dish also known as mud crab with chili sauce. Since then, eating had been primarily a utilitarian attempt to keep body and soul together while not getting sick. Scanning the limited late-afternoon menu, we both decided on a French Dip, then sat back and luxuriously drained our glasses of ice water—water from a pitcher, with ice, that you could actually drink! A sandwich materialized a few minutes later like a mirage, so perfectly did it fulfill my fantasy—meltingly tender filet mignon, sliced and laid on a lightly toasted and buttered baguette scored with grill marks, ideal for soaking up the neighboring cup of fragrantly meaty beef stock some *stagiaire* had been slaving over since morning. A bottle of syrupy Guinness provided the perfect complement. Was that French Dip truly the best sandwich I had ever tasted, or was hunger simply the best sauce? In any case, Jeremy sat back when he was finished, cocked an interrogative eyebrow at me, and just as the thought was forming in my mind, signaled for the waitress and said, "We'll have the same again." It was one of the things I loved about him, the uncanny flash of sympathy that divined I wanted to eat my "last meal" twice.

After a strained reunion, my husband and I joined Jeremy downstairs in the hotel lounge for drinks. Squaring off our awkward little triangle was Grant Abbott, a fellow attendee at the human rights conference, whom I had just learned would be accompanying us on the next leg of our trip. Grant seemed nice enough, earnest and well-meaning like most of the people Nathan worked with. Far more interesting was the queue of gorgeous women in skintight emerald cheongsams streaming into a room at the rear. What we guessed was a beauty contest turned out to be the interview process for Malaysia Airlines flight attendants. Our cocktail waitress, nearly as beautiful, was similarly attired in more muted silk, her dress so form-fitting it forced her to bend at the knees rather than the waist while serving drinks. My husband didn't seem to be interested in our stay with the Iban, a tribe who had given up headhunting so recently that some of the men bore tattoos boasting of decapitations they had performed, but Grant seemed eager to hear our traveler's tales. Jeremy told him about being tested by the chief on the six-foot blowpipe using darts formerly tipped with poison latex and about the blue kingfisher that flashed over our multicolored longboat on the river. By then, I had had a stiff drink, so I chose to recount an amusing if slightly inappropriate story.

I had contracted a painful urinary tract infection that grew steadily worse as we headed out of Pontianak into the rainforest. By the time our guide told us that the bus was approaching the last stop for picking up any necessities like batteries or rain ponchos, I had to raise myself off the seat every time we hit a bump in the road. I leafed through my Bahasa Malaysia dictionary for a translation of my ailment, but my heart sank as we pulled into what looked like the stage set for an old Western—a packed dirt street, one block long and lined with stores on both sides. I couldn't understand the signs, so I peered through the plate glass windows of each dim storefront until I spotted one whose shelves were lined with dusty apothecary jars. There were no lights on inside, but in the back two men were talking. I squinted up at the jars on the wall, hoping against hope that one of them contained powdered snakeskin or some local herb that could cure me. I shyly approached the counter at the rear and, in a desperate fit of courage, whispered "*pundi pundi empati*," which my dictionary translated as "bladder sick," but which I later learned means something closer to "gall bladder empathy." The man stifled a spasm of laughter and inquired in nearly Etonian English, "Is that Bahasa Malaysia?" When I nodded, he asked gently, "What seems to be the trouble?" I leaned over and whispered in his ear, not wanting the other man to hear. "Oh," he said, face brightening, "why didn't you say so? Want some sulfa drugs?" And he reached for one of the apothecary jars overhead and grabbed a handful of orange and yellow capsules, which he dropped into a small paper bag. Advising me to drink plenty of fluids, he charged me the equivalent of a dollar and kindly wished me good luck.

The waitress had been pouring Grant's beer when I got to "pundi pundi empati," and the bottle clattered against the rim of his glass as liquid sloshed onto the table. For a moment, we thought something was wrong with her. She had been so impeccably ceremonious until then. But a glance at her face showed that it was contorted with suppressed laughter, quickly replaced by horror that she had spilled something for perhaps the first time in her life. Apologizing profusely, she hurried off to find something to wipe away the evidence.

Her laughter had been contagious—Grant was still wiping his eyes—but my husband sat stony-faced. Was it that he disapproved of my story? Or did he mind that others thought it was funny? In the past, he had often kicked me under the table in similar circumstances—not hard, just enough to get me to shut up and to let me know that I would hear about it later—but this one was too low to the ground. My giddiness vanished; like the dress and pantyhose I was wearing, which felt so constricting after a week of shorts and sandals, this moment was a reminder of what I was so desperate to escape. I heard the cage click shut again and didn't say another word until it was time to go into the cocktail hour, where I ate hors d'oeuvres and felt Jeremy's eyes on me as I glad-handed like a politician's wife.

It was a relief the next morning to bust out of the Concorde Hotel after a fitful night and board the train to Port Klang with Jeremy. My husband was safely occupied in sessions until dinner, and by the time I boarded the high-speed ferry to Crab Island he was just a dull knot in my stomach. I can still feel the wind on my face as I sat in the prow of the boat, eyes closed, face tilted to the sun, letting the air sluice off the staleness of the previous twenty-four hours.

Crab Island—Pulau Ketam—is not really an island but a bizarre city on stilts, a series of interconnected boardwalks five feet wide that rise up out of a mangrove swamp in the middle of nowhere. Stepping onto the dock of the filthy fishing village was a shock after the shiny perfection of the city, but there was a paradoxical comfort in the dirt, only partly obscured by splashes of pink, blue, and yellow paint, the children bathing in tin washtubs, the stray dogs. They were a relief from the hard, unforgiving surfaces of the hotel, which I associated with the sense of restriction I felt there. On the other hand, lunching on the island's eponymous shellfish, which presumably emerged from the surrounding malodorous muck, would be going too far. We opted instead for the safety of a *roti canai* eaten with a plastic fork and washed down with soda straight from a glass bottle. A few hours of wandering on dead-end walkways induced in both of us a growing claustrophobia. There was something existentially horrifying about the place: an artificial structure built in the middle of nowhere, where there was no ground beneath your feet and literally nowhere to go. It felt like one of the settlements in *The Martian Chronicles*.

Nevertheless, I, at least, dreaded returning to the hotel. Kuala Lumpur, at least the "KL" of the international hotels, might as well have been New York—complete with husband. Nathan was in the room when I got back, giddy with freedom now that the conference was over. He had arranged for us to meet Grant for dinner at the American Graffiti Diner, where we ate burgers and fries surrounded by Malaysian businessmen excitedly calling each other on prototypes of Japanese cellphones, like boys with new walkie-talkies on Christmas morning. When we left to go bowling in the basement of a neighboring hotel, they were still at it, causing me to wonder why human rights workers, of all people, felt the need to relive our country's glory days in an Asian capital whose technology was apparently outstripping our own.

Our destination the next day was the Cameron Highlands, a favorite resort choice of British colonists beginning
in the late nineteenth century because its cool, rainy climate reminded them of dear old England. Why, I asked
my husband in a new spirit of open rebellion, would you
travel all the way to Borneo so you could go to Britain?
But the plans were already made, so we boarded a bus to
Tanah Rata. Three and a half hours later, we checked into
the rain-drenched Merlin Inn, a twin of the Econo-Lodge
I'd often passed on the Mass Pike. After dropping our bags
in a room that smelled troublingly of mold, we set off
under a mean drizzle to Ye Olde Smokehouse—neither
old nor a smokehouse—where we consumed a dispiriting
meal of fish and chips and steak pie. How had I never realized what a meat and potatoes guy he was? During the
entire trip, I don't think he ate one Malaysian dish. Our
considerable traveling during the previous decade had
been restricted to Europe, mostly to England, France, and
Italy. Even Greece had been too threateningly "foreign"
for him, although he was far too politically correct to
come out and say so. He panicked if he couldn't get a copy
of the *International Herald Tribune* (or the *New York Times* if
traveling in the United States), as if he needed proof that
the world continued to exist in his absence.

On the soggy walk back to the inn, it occurred to me
that there are two types of travelers: turtles and hermit

crabs. The turtle carries his identity with him wherever he goes, whether in the form of too much luggage or simply the desire to seek out the familiar. The hermit crab, on the other hand, travels precisely so he can discard his familiar persona and inhabit a fresh one in each new location. Nathan was a turtle, and I was experiencing for the first time the freedom of being a hermit crab. I felt resentful at being yanked forcibly back into my homely shell whenever I saw him. Sometimes I felt I was on two separate Malaysian trips, yo-yoing between them many times during a single day.

The next morning after breakfast we walked into Tanah Rata in the incessant drizzle. Every few minutes, a juggernaut thundering along Route 59 would force us onto the verge as it carted the rain forest away in triangular stacks of perfectly straight logs hundreds of feet long. There was nothing to buy and nothing to eat on the town's single commercial street, so Nathan decided to get a haircut in an ancient establishment Grant dubbed "The Barbershop that Time Forgot." As we awaited Nathan's turn in the mirrored room, Jeremy pulled out his camera and took a photograph of the four of us in the opposite mirror. When he snapped again, the flash went off, blindingly bouncing off all four walls, and we howled in protest. We were still blinking as Nathan burst from his chair into the street as if he'd been burned. The three of us stared after him in shock.

After a long moment, Grant said, "Someone should go after him."

When neither of us responded, he shook his head in polite disgust and went trotting off after Nathan, just visible at the bend of the Brinchang road.

I have held on to those photographs. The first shows Jeremy pointing his camera at the mirror, with me to his right, Nathan and Grant in profile seated along the adjoining wall. In the second, the flash obliterates Jeremy and me, and Nathan's face is turned toward the mirror, an unreadable expression on his face. Perhaps he had a flash of illumination, or maybe the reflection revealed something he could not face head on. In any case, those are the last images of our marriage.

Jeremy was uncharacteristically snappish on the walk back, and I could not distinguish between the gloom I felt inside and the weather without, but we found Nathan and Grant finishing a beer in the hotel's dark little bar as if nothing had happened. Dinner that night was an almost silent affair in a nearly empty dining room. Afterwards, Grant and Nathan went off to play billiards, and I escaped to bed. When I woke up the next morning, my husband had packed and gone. I descended to the dining room as if in a dream I could not shake off. Grant, sitting among the ruins of a protracted English breakfast, told me that Nathan had left him a note saying he'd flown home a day early. He asked for an explanation, but I just shook my head. What was there to say? It was pretty obvious what was happening, or was about to happen.

Jeremy and I left for the airport a few hours later, leaving Grant looking baffled and a little lonely, sheltering under the hotel portico from the perpetual rain.

I certainly can't condone my behavior, but after thinking about it for two and a half decades, I have come to understand it. I desperately wanted out of a prison partly of my own construction, and as a friend quipped when I returned home, "You took the express train." The same shortcomings that caused the problems in my marriage in the first place—fear of confrontation, inability to communicate, lack of self-knowledge—were those that prevented me from being able to end it with any sort of grace. If I had been capable of saying, "This relationship is strangling me. I am tired of being told what to do," I might not have had to leave. Jeremy's behavior, on the other hand, was harder to explain. Why didn't he take me aside when things got really ugly and say, "I can't stand torturing the poor bastard like this. I'll see you back in New York when you've figured this out"? Because Jeremy did not feel sorry for Nathan, nor did he see himself as a supporting player in my divorce. Everyone plays the lead in his own drama, and Jeremy's was a production of *Oedipus Rex* that had originated thirty years before in London, moved on to New York, and gone on tour briefly in Southeast Asia. I should have known he enjoyed the triangle from observing him in a similar configuration twice before. I should have realized he was a hermit crab who crawled into the shells of other people's marriages.

On our arrival at the terminal in Kuching, we were abruptly reminded again that we were foreigners, and far from home. The evening darkness seemed to press against the glass of the small waiting room, and throngs of people stared, transfixed and unabashed, at our light hair and eyes. One little girl, in her mother's arms, quickly reached out and touched my head as I walked by, withdrawing her fingers as if she'd brushed against something hot.

Our lodgings at the Anglican Hostel were so Spartan we quickly dubbed it the Anglican Hostile. The disapproving clerk at the reception desk, a dead ringer for Mrs. Danvers from *Rebecca*, somehow intuited we weren't married to each other despite my wedding ring. She almost refused to rent us even the separate rooms we requested but finally relented. The cavernous chambers had bare floorboards and were almost empty of furniture save a narrow bed covered with a white sheet pulled tight as a wimple. I brought the Scotch bottle and my toothbrush glass down to Jeremy's room. It was far too hot for sightseeing, so we stripped almost to our underwear and sank onto a couple of low wooden chairs. The lazy ceiling fan failed to disturb even the flame of the match I struck to light my cigarette. Eventually, we learned that if you stayed perfectly still, your skin cooled a little envelope a few inches around you. We drank and talked desultorily until the sun went down and the heat grew a bit less punishing. After years of marriage in which the topics to avoid had spread like a stain, the freedom of saying whatever came into my head was more intoxicating than the whisky. Retiring to our separate rooms after a simple dinner in town, I realized I was as happy as I'd ever been in my life. It was the happiness of the right-before, when everything is potential and no branch on the tree of possibility has yet been closed off by action.

The taxi driver assured us that the shadowy door thronged with scavenging, feral dogs was indeed the entrance to our hotel in Denpasar. The macabre light shed by the few sad Christmas bulbs drooping over the lintel made it look like a murder scene about to happen. Jeremy went to check if the inside was miraculously better but emerged looking pale. The driver motioned him over to the window, and Jeremy hopped back in looking cheerful. Apparently, there was a cousin with a hotel in Kuta. With the pessimism bred of a decade living in New York, I descended into sulky silence in which I imagined being pressured to stay at a hole in the wall worse than the one we just left but three times more expensive. Pulling up to an illuminated fountain at the end of a lushly planted drive ten minutes later, I saw—even in the dark—that I had been terribly wrong. The Kuta Puri Bungalows were way out of our league. We didn't even bother to get out of the taxi, which the driver kept running. He began a lengthy conversation with a man who appeared to be the owner, voices were raised, glances thrown in our direction. The driver returned, grinning. If we stayed for two nights, he said, the rate would be 36,000 Indonesian rupiah. We did some quick calculations—sixteen dollars. Only marginally higher than the fleabag in Denpasar. The sole catch was that only one bungalow was available. And so the final die was cast.

We didn't leave the room for two days. Platters of fruit with bottles of mineral water or pots of tea materialized by the door several times a day, conveyed by silent-footed bearers who later bore them away empty. Never again have I seen such beautiful fruit—vermilion papaya and scarlet watermelon. Slices of tiny pineapple and slivers of slippery jackfruit. Creamy miniature white and red bananas. Starfruit and mangosteens. Bizarre pear-shaped fruits covered in what looked like snakeskin. These were not meals so much as offerings. Instead of feeling the usual pressure from the cleaning staff to leave the room, we were distantly aware of a delicate respect for the privacy of what was going on behind our heavy wooden door. My thirty-first birthday passed in that hotel room, unnoticed.

Eventually, our bodies insisted on an actual meal. It was dark by the time we emerged into the mass of humanity thronging through Poppies Lane I, a narrow street lined with shops and restaurants only a few hundred yards from the hotel. It was shocking that such a bustle of life teemed just outside the sanctuary of the bungalow. We ducked into the nearest decent-looking *warung* and ordered *nasi goreng* and the special mushroom omelette from the menu chalked on the wall, along with a couple of Bintangs. I thought I was just being paranoid after not having seen a soul for two days, but I felt uneasy about how the waiters watched us as we began to eat. The *nasi goreng* was delicious, as always, but the omelette was surprisingly vile. Whatever varieties of wild mushroom they had in Bali bore no resemblance to those I'd had in the US or Europe, and I pushed the plate away after a couple of bites. Jeremy poked the omelette open and tried a bit of the filling, which he agreed tasted like dirt. We were discussing whether to send it back when I realized I felt odd. Someone kept adjusting the dial, making the light brighter and dimmer, sounds fainter and louder. Objects were too near and suddenly far away. We paid the check, and Jeremy half carried, half walked me back to the hotel. By the time we arrived, we had figured out that the "special" mushrooms had been psilocybin. We were idiots. By the time I started to feel normal again a few hours later, he had begun sweating and hallucinating, and because he had eaten more than I had, the rest of the night was spent putting wet washcloths on his head and reassuring him that the walls were not melting.

It would be hard to imagine two people who felt more ragged than those the shuttle bus deposited in Ubud the next morning, yet as soon as we turned off the Monkey Forest Road onto the verdant pathway to the Kubuku Bungalows, we began to feel restored. Ubud is preternaturally green, and therein lies its magic: it can restore you to greenness no matter how depleted you are. Within minutes, we were seated on a shaded platform overlooking rice fields stretching to a line of palm trees at the horizon. A cooling breeze intermittently set off the delicate tinkling of wind chimes carved to look like tiny farmers plowing the fields, their spinning blades designed to frighten away the birds. The brief intervals of silence were quiet in a way we had forgotten existed. When our server appeared and told us that the chimes were built by Wayan, the owner and chef, we were so distracted by his extraordinary appearance that we could hardly focus on what he said. A beautiful Balinese of indeterminate age, his bare chest smooth and coffee-colored above his sarong, his long nails filed into perfect almonds, he was androgynous not in an epicene way, like David Bowie or Patti Smith, but in a manner that seemed fully to embody both sexes. He was entirely charming and flirted with both of us, and soon we found we were speaking French with him, just for the fun of it. Then he brought us each a beer and left us alone. For once in my life, I felt completely content sitting there, neither wishing nor wanting for anything.

A few months before making this trip, Jeremy and I had seen a Japanese movie called *After Life* where each person, in the three days after death, had to choose a memory with which to enter eternity. They would reconstruct the scene, and when they truly remembered, with all their senses, their entire being, they would be launched into actual death. I guess in a way that meant that they could die happy. It had bothered me at the time that I could not choose a memory worth dying with or for, but in that moment in Ubud, I knew I had found it.

Later that day, we walked down the road to the Monkey Forest Sanctuary. True to its name, the Hindu temple complex was swarming with aggressively temperamental gray macaques, believed by the Balinese to protect against evil spirits. The Great Temple of Death, built of stone the color of sunset and carved with images of a demon goddess devouring children, made the hair on the back of my arms stand on end. Maybe the monkeys protected against evil spirits not by warding them off but by incarnating them, I suggested to Jeremy, like the Gadarene swine in the Bible. Walking back to the bungalows, I found myself thinking of "The Monkey's Paw," the short story in which the malevolent object of the title grants the owner anything he wishes for at a price he is not willing to pay. I wondered how far I would be willing to go to keep Jeremy.

We ate an early dinner that night in Wayan's restaurant, a platform suspended over the rice fields. Below, female farmers balanced huge baskets on their heads, walking with sinuous grace down paths that cut through the fields. The breeze blowing in smelled scrubbed, as if after rain. It was impossible to entertain dark thoughts in that place. I don't remember many particulars from that meal, aside from the fact that it was delicious, vegetarian, and for some reason we ate a lot of it with our hands. The one dish that I can taste in my memory is *urab sayur*. I think I recall it so clearly because I had been craving fresh vegetables, raw things, salad, which we hadn't eaten for almost two weeks because of a fear of getting sick. We had gotten by on cooked vegetables and peeled fruit, but they just weren't the same. I could have kicked myself for not having had a salad in Kuala Lumpur instead of all that heavy English and American food. Originally Javanese, *urab sayur* is essentially a cooked salad, crunchy and fresh. Blanched bean sprouts, sometimes shredded cabbage, and long beans (which look like overgrown string beans but have a denser texture) are tossed with grated coconut that has been spiced with chiles, garlic, kaffir lime leaves, and camphor-tinged *kencur*, a ginger-like root. It not only satisfied the craving but also relieved me of a feeling of guilt that had been instilled by my grandmother, who insisted that it was practically immoral if you didn't have at least one serving of "greens" daily.

After dinner, we went up to our room, if you could call a rustic platform raised on stilts above the rice paddy a room. Woven thatch on four sides could be rolled down for privacy (from the birds?), but we used only the mosquito netting, which bellied in and out with the evening breeze. The floor was almost entirely covered by a huge mattress, and we settled ourselves to read as the women left the fields for the evening, calling out their good nights. Only when the twilight faded from salmon to a peculiar pinkish gray did we realize the room had no electricity. It grew too dark to read, and I had just drifted off when I was jarred awake by a wall of sound that had broken through sleep like gradually worsening pain. The pleasant chirping of frogs and crickets had increased in volume to become an unbearable cacophony that was still, unbelievably, growing louder.

"My God, do you hear that?" I asked senselessly, since I could barely hear my own question.

Jeremy shrugged and turned over. He was a much more resilient traveler than I was.

I tried to imitate him by lying perfectly still, but the pandemonium hurt my ears. After a few minutes, I gave up and did my best imitation of the Nature Channel: "*The impressive mating sounds generated by the amphibious denizens of the* sawah *are a well-kept secret among the Balinese, who justly fear the negative impact on the tourist industry.*" Jeremy rolled on top of me, laughing, and pinned my wrists above my head, saying he'd be forced to take extreme measures unless I promised to be quiet. Later, we sat up, passing a cigarette back and forth. The frogs had finally quieted down, and I blurted out, "You know, I'm leaving Nathan whether things work out between us or not." It was the truth, but watching his face in the glowing ember of the cigarette, I realized it was precisely the wrong thing to say.

There were all sorts of reasons why my happiness on that trip was illusory—but does that make it any less real? We don't insist that pain be anchored in reality. Twenty-five years later, I can still summon the full force of the joy I felt during those weeks. Right before we broke up the following year, Jeremy said, "When I first met you, I thought you were the perfect woman." I fretted over that comment endlessly, wondering what failing he had unearthed after getting to know me, or in what fateful way I had changed. But eventually I put two and two together. Jeremy unmistakably began to lose interest the moment I told him I was leaving Nathan: the perfect woman was clearly one who belonged to someone else. I had thought I would do anything to keep him in my life, but there was one thing I was not willing to do—stay married. Everyone has to draw the line somewhere.

Urab Sayur

You can get all the ingredients except *kencur* easily in New York City, so I found and adapted a recipe that gets around it. I make this dish once in a great while when no one else is around, just to remind myself that I do understand what all the fuss is about—whether it was real or not.

Vegetables:
　　½ pound bean sprouts
　　½ pound long beans

Spice paste:
　　½ inch piece of peeled ginger
　　½ inch piece of peeled turmeric
　　½ inch piece of peeled galangal
　　1 chile pepper
　　1 shallot
　　3 cloves garlic

Remaining ingredients:
　　1 cup dried, unsweetened coconut
　　1 kaffir lime leaf
　　1 bay leaf

1 stick of crushed lemongrass
2 cups vegetable stock
salt and pepper to taste

1. Blend all of the ingredients for the spice paste in a small food processor.
2. Mix the spice paste with the dried coconut, kaffir lime leaf, bay leaf, 2 cups of vegetable stock, and lemongrass. Simmer and reduce until almost all of the water is gone. Add salt and pepper to taste. Remove from the heat and allow to cool.
3. Blanch the long beans and bean sprouts separately in a large pot of water. Remove and drain.
4. Just before serving, toss the seasoning mixture thoroughly with the vegetables.

Although this can be served hot or cold, I eat it at room temperature because that's how I remember it.

Serves: one if you're me; four if you're not.

is for

"Vegetarian"

My former husband was not a vegetarian, although he claimed to be. Technically, I suppose you would call him an "ovo-lacto-pescatarian" because he ate (within certain very limited parameters) eggs, dairy products, and fish. "Vegetarian" was wrong on two counts: not only did it suggest that he refrained from eating animal products, which he didn't, but it also suggested that he ate vegetables, which he rarely did. Although he tried to conceal it, he wasn't very fond of them. Needless to say, he was not pleased when I pointed this out, although his avoidance was so obvious that one night at dinner, after glancing at his father's plate, our young son announced, "Maybe I should become a vegetarian so I won't have to eat *my* vegetables."

Vegetables, however, were the least of the problems I faced when trying to decide what to cook for dinner. I used to fantasize about intercepting the *New York Times* in the morning and surreptitiously snipping out all the articles about health studies and food safety. I came to loathe these articles because I held them responsible for relentlessly reducing, over a period of decades, the number of foods my ex-husband considered safe to consume—to about five. Eventually, I came to think that "nutritional attritionist" was perhaps the most accurate way to describe him. When we first met, food was both my career and my avocation, and he was an avid diner-out. Our courtship took place over restaurant tables, and after we married, we entertained lavishly and often. Eating, both at home and abroad, was our primary shared recreational activity. But gradually, almost imperceptibly, our omnivore's Eden narrowed to a rabbit hole without the rabbit, which had gone the way of the lamb (scrapie, a variant of Mad Cow Disease), the veal (too cruel), the venison (parasites and prions), and the pork (trichinosis, vague religious scruples, and a horrifying *New York Times* story about a new disease transmitted by aerosolized pig brains at a meat processing plant). In a sort of reverse Noah's Ark, all were jettisoned, replaced by TVP (textured vegetable protein) in the shape of patties, meatballs, links, and riblets (in a box illustrated with a piglet holding a sign between its front trotters reading "Thanks!"). I started to feel like Charles Wallace Murry in *A Wrinkle in Time*, the only person at the table who can tell that the "delicious turkey dinner" served up by IT, the giant brain, is a sham and really tastes like sand.

Sushi had been a casualty of the late eighties, courtesy of a wedding my ex-husband attended with a bunch of gastroenterologists before I came on the scene (doctors being the only other source of reputable information besides the *Times*), and canned tuna had long been barred because of the high mercury content, but these were hardly encroachments on home cooking. Although there had been early signs of trouble in paradise, like the time he pronounced, "Eating a hamburger is like playing Russian roulette and waiting twenty years to find out if there was a bullet in the chamber," I still believed cooked fish and poultry would remain safe territory. Ah, love. Fresh tuna fell next—also a victim of mercury levels. Swordfish soon followed, verboten because of overfishing. Then farmed fish because of the PCBs. Oysters were deemed too risky because of the Norwalk virus, but once in a while, in a really good restaurant that he believed would test for it, he would still live dangerously and order half a dozen. Chicken was next, owing to the antibiotics used in raising them. ("What about antibiotic-free chicken?" I asked, when that became available. But once a food was banished it was never restored to grace.) It then became inevitable that turkey, as a matter of principle, would dwindle to a token serving at Thanksgiving. Duck, oddly enough, held on to the bitter end because he liked it, finally getting the boot only when he discovered "mock duck" made of— you guessed it.

The seas were calm during the early nineties until sustainability spread beyond swordfish. After that, I could prepare only seafood that had been given the little blue seal of approval by the Marine Stewardship Council, and since my ex-husband would only eat seafood that was both wild-caught *and* sustainable, that generally meant I had two choices: Alaskan wild salmon or Pacific (not Atlantic!) halibut. I did not inform him when Pacific halibut failed to make it onto the Monterey Bay Aquarium Super Green List of 2010. On the other hand, in double-checking the Marine Stewardship Council website the following year, my heart quickened to see a newly approved entry: krill, a delicacy I had, in my ignorance, believed was reserved for whales. But it was the humble sardine, he claimed, that was the perfect food: high in protein, low on the food chain, and never consumed by him despite his enthusiastic endorsement.

That my ex-husband generally followed recommendations as religiously as warnings posed its own set of problems. Was his permanently elevated blood level of mercury the result of faulty fillings or of eating fish four times a week for fifteen years after the *Times* reported that omega-3s were good for your heart? No matter which it was, we lived with the repercussions: Japanese food ceased to be a refuge from the food wars. California rolls had been a staple of his diet for decades since they are made with fake crab. Unfortunately, the fake crab is made from real fish, and the real fish is not always the relatively innocuous pollock. Some nosy reporter had to dig around and discover that it is sometimes made from shark, a predator high in mercury. Even the miso soup my ex-husband used to drink with the California roll was eventually banned: the dashi base is made from dried bonito flakes. The bonito is a small relative of . . . the tuna. And those tiny tofu cubes floating in the soup are not as innocuous as they seem: studies show that excess soy consumption increases estrogen production. A blood test was ordered to ascertain if they were safe to ingest.

The veggie patties that formed the staple of my ex-husband's diet, consumed in bulk and considered the ultimate "safe" food, contain the following ingredients:

TEXTURED VEGETABLE PROTEIN (WHEAT GLUTEN, SOY PROTEIN CONCENTRATE, SOY PROTEIN ISOLATE, WATER FOR HYDRATION), EGG WHITES, CORN OIL,

SODIUM CASEINATE, MODIFIED TAPIOCA STARCH,
CONTAINS TWO PERCENT OR LESS OF LACTOSE,
SOYBEAN OIL, HYDROLYZED VEGETABLE PROTEIN
(WHEAT GLUTEN, CORN GLUTEN, SOY PROTEIN),
AUTOLYZED YEAST EXTRACT, SPICES, NATURAL AND
ARTIFICIAL FLAVORS, SODIUM PHOSPHATES
(TRIPOLYPHOSPHATE, TETRAPYROPHOSPHATE,
HEXAMETAPHOSPHATE, MONOPHOSPHATE), SALT,
DISODIUM INOSINATE, CARAMEL COLOR, CELLULOSE
GUM, WHEY POWDER, MODIFIED CORN STARCH,
MALTODEXTRIN, POTASSIUM CHLORIDE, DEXTROSE,
ONION POWDER, DISODIUM GUANYLATE, VITAMINS
AND MINERALS (NIACINAMIDE, IRON [FERROUS
SULFATE], THIAMIN MONONITRATE [VITAMIN B1],
PYRIDOXINE HYDROCHLORIDE [VITAMIN B6],
RIBOFLAVIN [VITAMIN B2], VITAMIN B12), SUCCINIC
ACID, ASCORBIC ACID, LACTIC ACID, BREWERS YEAST,
TORULA YEAST, SOY LECITHIN.

The mind boggles at the number of logical inconsistencies here, given that he preferred to exclude from our home any fruit or vegetable raised by conventional agricultural methods, to say nothing of the house ban on nitrates, nitrites, hydrolyzed vegetable protein (which, along with autolyzed yeast extract, he called "stealth MSG"—perhaps he missed those in the fine print above), trans fats, and any food packaged in plastic. But I never seriously entertained calling him on the MSG, or all that soy, or the little plastic bags the patties were wrapped in. It just didn't seem fair to cut his daily caloric intake in half for the sake of making a point.

Of course, we owned no nonstick cookware (volatile compounds released at high heat), and he would not use the hot water from the Poland Spring dispenser in the kitchen (might have harbored harmful bacteria). Even the beloved Nalgene water bottles (#7 plastic) were tossed along with their special cleaner and brushes. He then switched to metal Sigg water bottles, which had to be ditched because of their BPA linings. Staying hydrated was a serious dilemma. Unfortunately, one can make even graver mistakes in the attempt to avoid chemical hazards. The hard plastic Aveeno bottles we insisted upon for our infant son turned out to be more dangerous than the classic soft ones we so assiduously avoided, causing us years of needless worry about early puberty.

To deflect the oft-repeated question, "Is it organic?" I perfected an extremely useful noncommittal grunt, inspired by a friend's father who, upon moving to Paris without learning which French nouns were feminine and which masculine, cleverly devised a sound exactly halfway between "le" and "la." But the day arrived when it no longer sufficed for fruits and vegetables to be merely organic. They had to be both organic and domestic. If imported from Mexico, news reports revealed that they might be contaminated with *E. coli* from improper hygiene or sanitation; if imported from farther afield, like Australia or South America, the huge carbon footprint offset any gains from the avoidance of pesticides. Recently the *New York Times* reported that rice—solace of invalids and sustainer of babes for centuries—readily absorbs toxic metals like arsenic and cadmium from the soil. The next day my ex-husband sent me a plaintive email that read, "See, there really is nothing left to eat."

One day toward the end of our marriage, I stood with my hands on my hips before an open cupboard trying to work up some enthusiasm for a box of quinoa and some raw cashews. I didn't hear him come in behind me. "Why don't you cook anymore?" he asked wistfully. I turned to face him, tempted to reply, "What do you expect me to serve, air sandwiches?" But I had lost my taste for tart ripostes. And really, by that time there was nothing left to say.

is for

White Truffles

When I was a young editor, I was charged with revising one of the most famous series of plays in English literature. It was a monumental job, and I was terrified, but I did manage to ascertain which scholar should be the series editor. The only problem was how to convince him to take it on. I flew to New Mexico to meet him at a conference, allowed him to dictate his terms, and drafted a contract that he dragged his feet about signing for months despite my obsequious and increasingly desperate letters and phone calls. Finally, the publisher told me to "get him in the office," even though it meant flying him and his chosen aide-de-camp across the country.

This scholar, a giant in one of the most snobbish fields in literature and a professor at one of the most illustrious universities in the country, was both brilliant and judgmental—the sort of person who makes you hear your own voice in your ears and find it nasal, inarticulate, and philistine. Like many such figures, however, he was engaged in a running battle with a rival—a Moriarty to his Sherlock Holmes—who corroded his soul with envy. The mention of this person's name caused a visible shudder to pass through his body. He was second to him, and only to him, and he and everyone else knew it. It didn't help that they shared a first name. Only because this other scholar had edited a similar project did we have any hope of getting him to undertake such a massive task.

On a crisp blue October day of the kind New York does best, the city air charged with promise and energy like negative ions after a thunderstorm, we walked the few blocks to Da Silvano, a deceptively simple Tuscan restaurant in Greenwich Village. Now shuttered, Da Silvano was a sort of celebrity canteen whose ocher and brick walls, tile floor, and windowed front wall opened onto a sidewalk café, the better to be seen behind enormous dark glasses. We sat inside, at a round table covered with a simple white cloth, in the sunny front room by the bar. The professor was unimpressed with our offer of a glamorous bottle of Ornellaia, which he turned down with a sniff, saying he wasn't interested in wine. I was starting to panic that I had wasted the publisher's money and everyone's time when the waiter announced the specials. "And this is the beginning of the season of *tartufo bianco*, the white truffle from Piedmont, which we will be serving over fresh tagliatelle." I don't remember what white truffles cost then, but now they are $3,000 a pound. I heard a sharp intake of breath and looked over at the professor, who, not wanting to appear greedy, tried to mask the excitement in his face. The publisher had noticed the same thing and gave me an all but imperceptible nod. "Go ahead," I said. "You should order it." (I was already rationalizing in my head that the price couldn't be much more than the bottle of Super Tuscan wine he had already turned down.) He demurred politely. The publisher insisted. He capitulated, happily defeated.

He was a hard man to talk to, even for the publisher, an urbane Englishwoman with exquisite taste in literature. Although he had not been willing to turn down a free trip to New York for himself and his colleague, he was determined not to be pleased. One conversational gambit after another petered out into awkward silence as we sipped Pellegrino and tried not to eat too much bread.

We smelled the waiter before we saw him. The white plate heaped with buttery golden tagliatelle that he set before the professor was beautiful. But we were transfixed by the enormous, odiferous, misshapen potato-like lump he picked up, along with a silver shaver, from the tray. Petals of truffle began to fall over the professor's plate, mixing with the steam of the pasta to form an aromatic cloud so overpowering it was almost obscene—those pheromones that drive the truffle pigs so wild made us steal glances at the other tables as if we were up to something shameful. The waiter seemed to go on forever, as when time slows almost to a stop during a car accident, joy and pain being so similar at the poles, he having looked inquiringly at the publisher and she having given him the nod to continue. Finally, he wished us a good appetite and we were able to exhale. The spell, the crazy suspense of the moment, was broken. The professor gazed at his plate for a long time. When he raised his head, his eyes were unfocused, blind to all of us. He looked down again quickly, and when he raised his head for the second time, his face was positively transfigured, his smile beatific, full of good will for the world and all its creatures, his eyes brimming with what looked like tears.

"I'm . . . so . . . happy," he said, his voice choked with emotion.

Later that afternoon, he signed.

is for

Xanthan Gum

When I was a cookbook editor, people often exclaimed, "Oh, I love cookbooks! I read them in bed, like novels." They expected me to be pleased, but the comment irritated me. I'm all for using one's imagination in bed, but my job was to ensure that the books I edited, especially those by chefs, were good for something besides escapist reverie. It was hard work protecting brave souls who actually ventured into their kitchens from the hidden pitfalls of these elaborate productions. How were they to know that one second of chef time equals one minute of civilian time, or that the ease with which a recipe can be imagined (helped along by drool-inducing photographs) is not at all proportional to the ease with which it can be executed?

I believed myself immune to these trickeries until, years after I left the business, I encountered an entirely new beast: the six-volume *Modernist Cuisine*. Nathan Myhrvold, the brains behind this leviathan, graduated from college at fourteen and collected a PhD in mathematical physics along with a couple of masters degrees by the time he was twenty-three, eventually retiring as Microsoft's first chief technology officer at forty. Then he founded his own company and settled down to produce his magnum opus. I was delighted to receive his coveted behemoth from my husband for Christmas in 2011. Risking a herniated disc, we heaved it onto the digital bathroom scale, where it weighed in at forty-three pounds. As soon as the holiday hubbub quieted down, I put Volume 1 on my lap and started reading until my legs fell asleep. While I didn't really hope to plow straight through the set's 2,438 pages, it seemed disrespectful to flip through the *Larousse Gastronomique* of a parallel universe as if it were a glossy magazine. *History and Fundamentals* was heavy on food safety, and Myhrvold nearly lost me midway at the chapter on Parasitical Worms, with its revoltingly enlarged photos of tapeworms and live flukes emerging from pieces of halibut bought at the fish store, but the survival instinct propelled me forward to the charts on thermal death curves. The day I started Volume 2, *Techniques and Equipment*,

I got a call that my mother was in the ICU, the catalyst in a series of events that would explode my family, both nuclear and extended. The glossy tome lay open on the floor where it had fallen, collecting dust, before someone finally slipped it back into its plexiglass case. It would be four years before I took it out again, from a different bookshelf this time, in a different apartment.

Paging through the spiral-bound Volume 6 on that frigid January day, I felt something akin to wanderlust. The recipes adumbrated a world whose inhabitants sustained themselves on citrus air, ultrasonic fries, pineapple glass, spiced ash, fossilized salsify branch, and edible prune coals. It was slightly creepy that some instructional photographs in the other volumes featured syringes and blue-green surgical gloves, and that pasta in this alternate universe took the form of gel noodles extruded by a peristaltic pump, but I had been fascinated by the intersection of science and cooking since I received a chemistry set and an Easy-Bake Oven for Christmas when I was nine and attempted to use them together. In fact, that was my only faint similarity to Myhrvold, who had tried at the same age to flambé his family's Thanksgiving turkey under the influence of *The Pyromaniac's Cookbook*. I was soon to be harshly reminded that, among our many differences, he is both a trained scientist and a trained chef. (In the interstices of his Microsoft career, Myhrvold had found time to cook in some high-end restaurants and earn a diploma from the École de Cuisine La Varenne.)

In his book *Stumbling on Happiness*, Daniel Gilbert analyzes the ways in which we deceive ourselves about the future. We use our imaginations to look into time just as we use our eyes to look into space, he observes, warning that the mind's eye can be tricked by a specimen of optical illusion when visualizing possible outcomes. *Modernist Cuisine*, whether intentionally or not, lays a number of traps for the imagination, and I blundered into every one.

First, I fell prey to the hyperreality of the photographs. Bob Tuschman, head of programming for the Food Network, described the secret of food porn as blowing up the image so that you can see its "pores," evoking a primitive desire to "bring it back to your cave." *Modernist Cuisine* elevates food porn to a new level, and the only way to slake the desire aroused by these photographs is to reproduce what is on the page. I misapprehended that since an image seemed so real I could taste it, it must be possible to make it. Second, I was duped by what I came to call the Dimensional Fallacy: because a recipe fits on a single page, it must take no time at all to execute. I discovered the hard way that it is an error of logic to assume that the amount of space occupied by two dimensions has anything to do with the amount of time occupied by four. These recipes took up so little room not because they were brief but because they were printed single-spaced in a minuscule font on a huge page with tiny margins. As a final snare, the compression of the language rivals that of the layout. The instructions are a model of clarity and concision, written in a scientific shorthand devoid of the usual explanations and encouragements. I should have realized I was looking not at recipes but at lab notes, and that my point of comparison should have been a textbook rather than a cookbook. In short, I should have taken Ferran Adrià's introductory comment that the book is "not easy, yet clear" as a warning rather than as a gnomic pronouncement.

As yet happily unclear as to *why* the book was not easy, I became fixated on the adaptation of Adrià's Mussels in Mussel Juice Spheres (Volume 4, page 191), which looked like crystalline jellyfish washed up on the beach after a storm. For days, I stared at the picture in a sort of trance as I painstakingly followed the recipe's instructions in my mind. I could almost feel the orbs dissolve on my tongue, releasing the brine into my mouth. I told myself I experienced nearly as much satisfaction from going through the mental process as if I had actually done it, but I couldn't banish the pesky image of someone confined to bed who thinks she can keep up her tennis game by practicing her serve in her mind. Who was I fooling? I was not going to purchase or contrive a sous-vide apparatus to prepare mussel jus from rock mussels, mollusks that an Internet search suggested I would find only in the Dravanian Forelands of an online role-playing game called *Final Fantasy XIV*. And in fact I had no idea what the final product of the spherification process would taste like. So I decided to find a recipe that used some of the space-age ingredients that appealed to the frustrated chemist in me but that I could actually execute in the real world.

In the end, I decided on Adrià's Liquid Pimento Olives, which appear a few pages later. I wanted to try reverse cryospherification, and deconstructing and reconstructing an olive seemed doable. Even though I am not a martini drinker and had no use for pseudo-olives, they were at least theoretically edible, unlike the recipe for fake raw egg on the following page, perhaps intended as a (literal) magician's gag. And they contained three of the mysterious powders I longed to use: sodium alginate, calcium lactate, and xanthan gum.

I read up on these a little, and only xanthan gum gave me pause. The product of fermenting sugar with *Xanthomonas campestris*, the mold that produces those nasty black spots on broccoli, xanthan gum is also used in wallpaper glue and oil drilling because of its frankly slimy properties. In fact, another modernist cooking manual warns, "adding too much xanthan gum can result in a texture and mouthfeel resembling mucus." But Myhrvold reassures that this product of microbial fermentation is "just as natural as vinegar and yeast." It seems silly to have gotten nervous about an ingredient that has since made its way onto *The Great British Baking Show*, but it would be several years before the passion for gluten-free baking brought xanthan gum out of the laboratory and onto the supermarket shelf beside the King Arthur flour. In any case, perhaps the lesson is that you can't win. You think something is suspicious for one reason (nasty white chemical) and find out it's actually suspicious for quite another (nasty black mold). As for sodium alginate (made of seaweed) and calcium lactate (those crystals that form on your cheese), they were clearly harmless.

Liquid Pimento Olive

Modernist Cuisine

(Adapted from Ferran Adrià)

INGREDIENT	QUANTITY	SCALING
Extra-virgin olive oil	500 g	100%
Thyme	20 g	4%
Orange peel, julienne	15 g	3%

1. Combine to make aromatic olive oil.
2. Reserve for later use.

INGREDIENT	QUANTITY	SCALING
Green olives, pitted	500 g	100%
Olive brine, from olives	200 g	40%

3. Blend in food processor to fine paste.
4. Press through fine sieve, and reserve 450 g of olive puree.

INGREDIENT	QUANTITY	SCALING
Calcium lactate	13.5 g	2.7% *(3%)**

5. Blend by hand with olive puree until completely dissolved.

INGREDIENT	QUANTITY	SCALING
Xanthan gum (Texturas brand)	1.6 g	.32% *(0.36%)**

6. Blend gradually with olive puree.
7. Cast into hemisphere molds.

INGREDIENT	QUANTITY	SCALING
Piquillo pepper, cut in thin strips (store-bought)	15 g	3%

8. Place pepper strip on top, and carefully push into each hemisphere.
9. Freeze.

INGREDIENT	QUANTITY	SCALING
Sodium alginate (Algin, Texturas brand)	5 g	1%
Water	1 kg	200%

10. Disperse with hand blender, and refrigerate until needed.
11. Before use, blend until sodium alginate is completely incorporated.

12. Vacuum seal to remove accumulated bubbles.

13. Pour into bowl to make bath for setting olives.

14. Bring bath to simmer.

15. Remove each frozen hemisphere from mold, place on spoon, and tip gently into bath.

16. Set in bath for 3 min. Hemispheres will thaw into spheres, and skin will form.

17. Remove olive sphere from bath with perforated spoon.

18. Rinse sphere twice in cold water.

19. Repeat with remaining olive hemispheres.

20. Store spherified olives, refrigerated, in reserved aromatic olive oil.

(% of weight of reserved olive puree)

Yield: 480 g

Day 1: Before beginning, I search the Internet for afford-
able molecular gastronomy ingredients. In the interest of
economy, I decide to purchase a used *Modernist Pantry* kit
on eBay, disregarding the recipe's stipulation of Texturas
brand xanthan gum and sodium alginate. This one-stop
shopping option includes packets of all the chemicals I
need (plus many I don't) along with a special perforated
spoon and a digital scale sensitive enough to measure dust.
I should have heeded that the seller had opened exactly
one of the envelopes (sodium alginate) before giving up;
she was even throwing in a free twenty-five dollars silicone mold of the kind I needed for the olive spheres.

Day 2: While awaiting delivery, I prepare the aromatic
olive oil. The process is suspiciously easy, and I have a
feeling of foreboding that it is all downhill from here.

Day 3: Still awaiting delivery, I walk to Zabar's to buy
piquillo peppers, otherwise known as pimentos, and green
olives. Thwarted in my attempt to collect olive brine with
the olives I purchase, I am forced to buy a huge additional
can just for the salt water. (No way am I jeopardizing this
recipe by using the inferior canned olives themselves.)
Weighing the olives and the brine discloses that the label
vastly overrepresents the weight of the former and under-
represents the weight of the latter. This is probably not an

isolated occurrence, but I doubt most people drain their canned food and compare the relative weight of the wet and dry contents. Even if they did, what recourse would they have for olives imported from Syria, which has more pressing concerns than customer-service complaints?

Day 5: The kit arrives late in the afternoon. I open it immediately and prepare the sodium alginate solution. An intensive Google search suggests that refrigerating for twenty-four hours will banish bubbles in lieu of the $700 chamber vacuum sealer hiding in Step 12.

Day 6: I haul out the ancient food processor the next day with a feeling of anticipation, but my confidence evaporates almost instantly when I begin to press the olive paste through a fine sieve. Instead of a glossy "puree," only dun-colored water drips through. This can't be right, so I switch to a slightly coarser sieve. The result looks thick and creamy, more like pea puree, but I am a bit concerned when the yield is at least four times the expected 450 grams. Referring back to the illustrated volume (I have been using the spiral-bound recipe book designed for the kitchen), I notice with a pang of dread a hand pouring green liquid into a mold. I try liquefying my puree with an immersion blender, but it refuses to approach the consistency in the picture. My misgivings deepen when I further thicken my puree with the xanthan gum, yielding a bowlful of wobbly olive batter, which I spoon rather than "cast" into the molds. The last step resembles a gluey game of Operation, where I use tweezers to place a tiny piece of pimento in the center of each circle. After putting my tray of fifteen olives into the freezer, I am left with enough mixture for hundreds more. As the days pass, my olive oil has darkened ominously while remaining stubbornly unaromatic.

Day 7: Significantly less optimistic, I return to the kitchen in the morning to heat the sodium alginate solution, immediately releasing all of the bubbles I sought to eliminate with refrigeration. Worse, the temperature of the solution refuses to rise above 185 degrees even after an hour on the stove. Some chefs say a simmer can be as low as 180 degrees, so I give up and lower the first suspiciously sturdy disk into the bath with the special perforated spoon and wait for it to blossom magically into a sphere. Nothing happens. I set the timer for one minute. Still nothing. Two minutes, three, four. Defeated, I fish it out, dunking it in two cold baths and letting it drain a moment. It resembles a slick, khaki-colored flying saucer. I bite down cautiously, and a rush of clear goo squirts from the middle, followed by a mouthful of curdled olive jelly. It is a good thing I am standing over the sink. I nibble the edge of a frozen disk, awful in a different way—dense and alkaline—before emptying the silicone tray and refrigerated puree into the trashcan. At least I can salvage the olive oil, since it tastes of . . . olive oil.

Post mortem: It was pretty easy to diagnose what went wrong. Although I had practically memorized the instructions, I'd missed a nearly invisible photo caption that read, "The ideal viscosity is that of thick cream." I'd lost my nerve when what was essentially brine dripped from the sieve, thinking I was aiming for a vegetable puree rather than an "edible liquid." (Am I wrong in thinking that the need to use "edible" in a cookbook is a red flag?) Perhaps I compounded my error by using generic xanthan gum and sodium alginate. And as for those mysterious reappearing bubbles in the sodium alginate solution, I must have overlooked somewhere in those 2,438 pages what I discovered too late elsewhere: that I was supposed to use distilled water. But in the final analysis, I was the victim of a chemical paradox: my mixture was too thick to round into a sphere. In any case, upon rereading my entries, I recognize a pattern all too familiar from diaries throughout history: the path from infatuation to disillusionment.

As always, however, there are lessons to be gleaned from heartbreak. I had become so obsessed with producing something—anything—that would gain me access to this esoteric realm that I wasted a week of my life trying to produce a garnish for drinks I never intended to serve. What I lost sight of during the process was the most important ratio of all: that of effort to reward.

is for

Yquem

It is a truth universally acknowledged, that a divorced woman in search of a good husband must be in want of a life. That is to say, if you are to avoid repeating the mistakes you made the last time, you must learn how to live by yourself, to like your own company, and to stand on your own two feet, so that when you finally choose a mate, you will be "two solitudes that meet, protect and greet each other," in Rilke's lofty phrase, rather than a co-dependent mess. At least this is what I told myself when I found myself divorced and living in a shabby basement apartment in Brooklyn at thirty-one. I was so desperately afraid of being alone, so terrified that without someone to witness my existence I would actually die, that at least once an evening I would find myself with the phone in my hand about to call someone, anyone, to arrange a disastrous rendezvous. But I had a wise best friend and a good therapist, both of whom advised me that the only way out was through, and assured me that the existential terror would pass if I just sat still long enough to tolerate it. And so I folded myself up in a battered wing chair night after night, staring at the Duraflame log in the fireplace, smoking cigarettes and sipping Scotch until it was time to put myself to bed. Slowly, I learned how to live in my own skin.

After three seasons of introspection and enforced celibacy, I went to a New Year's Eve party. The tarot-reading psychic in the cloakroom gave me a forgettable reading, then urgently whispered a piece of dubious advice in my ear as I stood to leave: "Wear pink underwear if you want to meet someone!"

All night I had been uncomfortably aware, each time I turned my head, of the stare of an intense-looking man in a cardigan. The cardigan somehow made the stare even more unsettling. He turned out to be a friend of the hostess, who called the next day, promising he wasn't a serial killer and asking if it was all right to give him my number. What the hell, I thought. It was cheaper than buying all new underwear.

One thing I learned from the disastrous year that followed is that there is not as much correlation as there should be between the depth of your feeling for someone and how much he can make you suffer. You can know that he is all wrong for you, that you are temperamentally incompatible, you can even feel superior to him in just about every way, and still, if you are a romantic obsessive by nature, you can use him to make yourself miserable. I am like the little bird in *Are You My Mother?*, programmed to latch onto the next available love object, no matter how inappropriate. So my nine months in front of the fire, while not exactly wasted, were not as salutary as I had hoped they would be.

When we had been dating for about two months, he asked me to go dancing. I hate dancing. I'm bad at it and, if still sober enough to be coordinated, I can never remember to smile and pretend I'm having a good time. But it was in that early stage of a relationship where you will (if you are me) seriously consider things like participating in a Harley rally when getting on the back of a motorcycle is one of the few things you have sworn never to do to in your life, so of course I agreed. After a few excruciating hours during which he repeatedly asked if my shoes were hurting, he invited me back to his apartment for the first time.

We stood for ages in the bitter March wind trying to find a cab. The tiny black Azzedine Alaïa knockoff that had seemed sexy in the dance club felt merely inadequate now. I was chilled to the bone by the time we arrived at his Greenwich Village apartment, which was hardly warmer than the street, but I was too vain to keep my jacket on and let him hang it in his frighteningly tidy closet. I followed him into the kitchen, but he told me to go sit on the couch and look pretty. Like all his compliments, this one had an irritating tinge of masculine condescension that I chose to ignore.

I looked around for a throw or even a few pillows to pile on myself for warmth, but the living room was a severely tailored, charcoal gray and black affair, relieved only by a stunning view of the Empire State Building. The upholstery on the sofa was stretched so tight you could bounce a quarter on it, and I noticed with amusement that the pillows actually buttoned up. I stepped out of my vertiginous heels and curled up in a corner of the couch, pulling my stretchy dress over my knees for warmth and piling the two pillows on my lap. At last he emerged, set a tray on the coffee table, and began lighting candles and adjusting dimmers with the touching finickiness of someone who hasn't entertained in a long time. The tray held a slab of foie gras, pale pink and rimmed with bright yellow fat, studded with a black truffle. There were some triangles of toast in a linen-lined basket, which I was tempted to use as a hand warmer. And there were two delicate glasses and a half-bottle of Chateau d'Yquem 1985. Even I knew the name of the legendary dessert wine unanimously agreed to be the apotheosis of Sauternes.

"Wow," I said. "Yquem."

"Don't get too excited," he replied. "It's not a very good year."

He explained that the 1985 vintage went well with foie gras because it lacked some of the vineyard's characteristic complexity.

The lighting finally arranged to his satisfaction, he sat down next to me and poured a drop of the yellow-gold wine into a glass, swirled, and sipped. He grimaced and held it out to me. I knew enough after a few dates to take it by the stem.

"This wine is way too cold," he said sternly, as if I were somehow to blame for his having stored it in the refrigerator. "We have to wait for it to warm up. Besides, it's just a baby. It needs at least another ten years."

I felt chastised again, as if I were a naughty child too impatient to sit for another decade and wait for the wine to age properly. His denigration of the wine's vintage, age, and temperature left me utterly unprepared for the shock of that first mouthful, so sublime that tears pricked at my eyes. Sensations and associations flooded through me as I held it on my tongue—honey, yes, and honeysuckle, and the smell of peach cobbler bubbling over in my grandmother's oven, and a bite of tarte Tatin—grounded by an austere elegance that tamed the sweetness into subservience. I was pierced with a great tenderness for my life, the interconnected world, this man I hardly knew—and a deep longing. And all that was before I swallowed. When I did, the experience of the wine persisted, miraculously intact. This was a *bad* year?

"It just goes on and on," I said wonderingly.

"That's the finish," he responded briskly, but his eyes were still gentle from watching my reaction. As he gave me a little lecture on *botrytis*, the noble rot that dessicates the Sémillon grapes into such unearthly sweetness, he refilled our glasses and handed me a triangle of toast thickly topped with foie gras. "Now taste it with this." It was a pairing I had only read about and had been dying to try for years.

At some point, the lights in the Empire State Building went off, unobserved, and the sky turned the color of stone behind it. The candle flames were nearly invisible in the non-light of almost-morning. The bottle, having performed its magic, was empty. Suddenly self-conscious, we sat up. I adjusted my dress. He smoothed his hair. Wordlessly, he helped me on with my jacket. What was there to say? The people standing awkwardly by the door were not the people on the sofa.

Hurrying to the subway station, the vicious wind off the Hudson swirled up and around my exposed legs. I felt I had been dropped from a great height and was scurrying, insignificant as an insect, beneath an enormous and uncaring sky. It may seem silly that a glass of wine could be the vehicle for such an experience, but the needle of the sublime, which leaves a hole where it enters and where it emerges, can be threaded with any beauty.

is for

Zucchini Blossoms

Although his plots were measured in square feet rather than acres, my grandfather insisted that he was a farmer, not a gardener. After mulling this over for decades, I finally realized he meant that he was interested not in the act of gardening but in the results, the product, the produce. (Certainly, he never wasted his time on flowers.) He was not self-conscious enough to derive pleasure from performing the actions of preparing the soil, planting, pruning, weeding, and harvesting, like some Edwardian lady in a large hat wielding secateurs. Although it was an avocation and he enjoyed it, much as he liked playing golf or listening to baseball on the radio, he treated gardening like a business. It was natural to him. He had grown up on a farm in southern New Jersey, near Hammonton, the blueberry capital of the country, one of eleven children of Italian immigrants. His earliest memory was of being turned out of bed when he was no more than four years old and sent into the blueberry fields with the rest of the family to pick off an infestation of beetles that had descended during the night. Having been a human pesticide, he was not about to forgo the miracle of chemicals. If it was a question of who was going to eat his vegetables—him or the bugs—it was going to be him. He was equally profligate with fertilizer. There was no such thing as an unfair advantage in the battle against nature. It was like hunting for food as opposed to for sport, even though the days were long gone when a family needed to subsist on what he grew. He was utterly unsentimental about his plants, pruning and thinning them almost sadistically, or so it appeared to us until the new growth sprang forth from the ugly hacks he had made with shears or saw.

My grandfather's was the story of a generation: the son of immigrant parents, a printer by trade, he made good by dint of hard work coupled with the lucky breaks provided by World War II and the prosperous years that followed. By the time I knew him, he had two houses, one by the ocean, each with a garden. His tomatoes flourished; his Boston lettuce was baby-tender; but it was zucchini, which flourishes under a thumb far less green than his, that turned into a vegetable plague each summer, inflating under the influence of Miracle-Gro to cartoonish proportions seemingly overnight. Eating the blossoms was a delicious form of birth control; we had to nip the problem in the bud or be buried in a pile of squash from which even my grandmother's culinary ingenuity could not rescue us.

Any summer morning in Avalon, New Jersey. I pull on some shorts and hurry outside the moment I wake up. It is exciting and private, the world before sunrise, when the ground is cold beneath my feet and the porch railings drip with salty moisture. No one has breathed this air but me. It has blown across thousands of miles of ocean, straight from Europe. The island is hushed, and if I strain my ears, I can hear the surf, never audible during the day. A laughing gull perched on a nearby telephone pole sends up its eerie dying caw. Then the sun, hot on my cheek, evaporates the mystery. The smell of Barbasol and the sound of running water through the bathroom window signal the imminent appearance of my grandfather. My grandmother is whistling in the kitchen (how unlike my mother she is). A minute later the screen door bangs softly, and I run to the side of the house to help her gather zucchini blossoms in her terrycloth apron before they open. Back inside, the breeze flutters the yellow half-curtains above the kitchen sink as she peers carefully inside each flower to check for unwanted guests, then showers it gently with the black nozzle and lays it on a bed of paper towels. Later that morning, when the blossoms are quite dry, she heats half an inch of Wesson oil in a frying pan and whips up the batter, which is both a heresy and a miracle. This ethereal, inimitable batter, never to be equaled, is a very thin decoction of water and . . . Bisquick.

I am standing at her elbow now as she twirls a blossom in the batter and gives it a quick shake. The fritter sizzles as it hits the hot oil, and she waits for delicate bubbles at the periphery to signal it is time for the single turn. Then she waits again for the incomparable gold to appear, a gold like a child's downy forearm in the sun. Tipped from the spatula onto a bed of more paper towels, most of the fritters never reach the table, disappearing when she turns back to the frying pan.

To this day, deep into middle age, I have never given up, ordering zucchini blossoms whenever they appear on a menu in their evanescent season. They arrive greasy and sodden, sometimes filled with cheese (lily-gilding) or with the miniature squash still attached, sprouting from the flower like a deformed thumb. Conversely, in a misguided attempt to achieve lightness, the blossoms will have been chopped up, resulting in something light but utterly characterless. But, of course, I am being unfair. No rendition, no matter how exquisite, could deliver the tang of the sea breeze through the screen door, the rustle of my grandfather's newspaper, the friendly sizzle of the pan, the ever-hopeful gulls shifting from foot to foot on the neighbor's slanted roof. It is a mystery how a humble fritter, a battered flower, can carry such a freight of sense memory— no, make that love.

Afterword

Food continues to surprise me with its infinite adaptability as living metaphor. On a recent trip to Vietnam with a few friends, I got a taste of how it can unite the foreign and the familiar in much the same way it fuses past and present. A monsoon was sweeping the coast, but we showed up for our street food tour in Hoi An anyway. Our guide, a young local named Phuoc, wasn't at the coffee shop where we were supposed to meet at three p.m., and it took another half hour for him to appear after the girl behind the counter called him on his cell phone. Although he tried to look pleasant as he tucked in his rumpled shirt and smoothed his hair, it was pretty clear he thought we were crazy for not canceling like everybody else. The skies had darkened steadily and the rain turned to sheets while we were waiting, but we gamely followed him into the lane, fording the streaming gutters outside the front door. Our misgivings deepened as we left the tourist precincts of the "Old Town" and splashed in silence behind him, our umbrellas nearly useless in the slanting deluge, the streets becoming more dilapidated until the buildings gave way entirely to empty stretches of mud.

After half an hour ankle-deep in cold rain, blindly following a stranger into no-man's-land, the tour no longer seemed like such a lark. We stopped to confer and decided to mutiny, but as we turned to announce our intention, we saw him vanish through what appeared to be a solid wall. Scurrying to catch up, we spotted an opening so narrow we had to furl our umbrellas before plunging into the Vietnamese version of Harry Potter's Diagon Alley. Our Western frames were too wide to permit facing forward, so we edged along obliquely while people stared down from their windows before resuming their conversations above our heads, as though we were tromping through their living rooms, which in some cases we basically were. Phuoc slipped ahead easily through the muddy warren, pausing at each turn for us to catch up. After countless labyrinthine twists, the light abruptly brightened and the roofs fell away, and we burst into a teeming city, buzzing with motorbikes and buses and bicycles. Here, behind the Potemkin Wall of UNESCO tourist stalls and pedestrian malls, was where the workers of Hoi An and their families actually lived.

Expertly dodging traffic, Phuoc led us to a street vendor stirring a cauldron of what looked like used motor oil. The tiny ceramic cups we were offered held black sesame soup, and Phuoc confided fondly that generations of schoolchildren had been kept "regular" by a daily morning dose from this very stall. In fact, the current vendor had taken over for her father when he turned one hundred. The soup was surprisingly delicious despite its off-putting appearance—smooth and slightly sweet—and miraculously warming. Somewhat fortified, we continued our pilgrimage, stopping in one open-fronted garage to taste a lady's famous green papaya salad and in a second to sample another's Cao Lau, the noodle dish unique to Hoi An. Then it was on to a covered alley for rice congee studded with cubes of congealed pig's blood and chunks of offal. Probably calibrating that our senses needed a rest, Phuoc chose for our next stop an elaborate multistory restaurant-*cum*-factory producing Hoi An's specialty: delicately translucent white rose dumplings. A table ringed with slim young girls was turning out small mountains of them, two-inch rounds of rice flour filled with a dime-sized bite of ground pork or shrimp. The proprietress who oversaw production was dressed in head-to-toe leopard Lycra despite her generous proportions, and every time our guide called her "Big Boss," she squirmed with pleasure and jangled her charm bracelets.

Drier now, and in a better mood after a plateful of dumplings and some tea, we splashed back into the street. Phuoc pointed out a woman selling fetal duck eggs as we passed her on the curb, not bothering to pause as he asked if anyone was willing to try one. When two of us surprised him by saying yes, he gave his first real grin of the day and suggested we allow the vendor to prepare them for us. Of course we agreed, deciding not to observe the proceedings too closely. There's a reason eating a fetal duck egg is one of the stunts on *Fear Factor*, and what the eye doesn't see, the gorge doesn't rise over. A few minutes later, my egg was peeled, sauced, and being held out on a large ceramic spoon by the smiling vendor. I opened my mouth, and she popped it in as if I were a finicky toddler. I had no choice but to chew and swallow, but suffice it to say that fetal duck eggs in Hoi An are matured for nineteen to twenty-one days, and embryos begin to develop beaks and feathers at seventeen days. It was a relief a few minutes later to detect the familiar smell of roasting pork and join some teenage girls giggling around roadside braziers as if they were tables at Pinkberry. Although we had been eating for hours, we happily accepted a palate-cleansing kebab on a chopstick.

We still had one more garage to visit, though, where Phuoc told us we were to learn the art of sucking snails. He was greeted like a member of the family, which perhaps he was, and we were seated on the ubiquitous child-sized plastic chairs. A few minutes later, Phuoc carried over a mounded bowl of *oc hut*, small dark snails in a sea of red chili sauce. The idea, he said, was to pick them up and suck the meat out of the larger end. If nothing happened— and for us nothing did—you were supposed to suck the pointy end to break the seal and try again. The technique was much trickier than you might expect, and our hands and lips were on fire by the time we finally got the hang of it. Our pleasure in succeeding was offset by the discovery that the large end was covered by a crunchy, keratinous little plug that had to be chewed and swallowed, while the snail meat tasted like mud. At our last stop, we joined a queue of children dancing with impatience as they awaited their after-school snack: individually made fish-shaped waffles, like Japanese *taiyaki*, redolent of vanilla and stuffed with bean paste or chocolate.

At the end of the tour, Phuoc shared wistfully that his dream was to see New York City, but for me, going home was depressing. Vietnam's colors and flavors were so intense they made the city in January seem like a black-and-white movie; every morning I felt like Dorothy waking up in Kansas after clicking her heels in Oz. But lying in bed one day, long after I should have gotten up, in the middle of fantasizing about how to become an expat in Hanoi, I recalled the message of the movie: after running away, Dorothy ends up discovering "there's no place like home." Now it hit me why the sesame soup in Hoi An had seemed somehow familiar: in color and purpose, it was identical to the stewed prunes my grandmother had pressed upon me at various times during my youth. I had put up a token fuss because I knew I was supposed to, especially given what they were "for," but I actually liked their silky black sweetness. How was the age-old Chinese remedy any different from its homely Italian equivalent?

Food allows us to assimilate what is "foreign" and literally make it part of ourselves. When we swallow something like a fetal duck egg, we signal not only to others but also to ourselves that we are open to new experience. By ingesting a part of the culture that seemed unpalatable or even inedible only moments before, we are accepting an aspect of the people as well. Once you have gotten rid of the "*that*" in "They eat *that*?" there is no longer a "they." Just as profoundly, however, such openness can reveal that the seemingly foreign is simply home in a different guise. One twist of the kaleidoscope, and the sucking snails could be piles of blue crabs on a checked tablecloth in Avalon, the rice congee with pork my grandmother's Sunday spaghetti sauce crowded with sausage, meatballs, and *braciole*.

For Phuoc, the food tour had been merely a visit to the old neighborhood. Hoi An was Kansas for him, which meant New York was Oz. I didn't have to move to Hanoi to get the color back in my life. I only needed to wake up.

Acknowledgments

Heartfelt thanks to Carol Schneider, my "Dear Reader," who got every nuance and sent me back to the drawing board when she didn't. No words are adequate to express my gratitude to Wendy Wolf—secret weapon, dearest friend. The keenness of her vorpal blade is matched only by the warmth of her heart, and it will take another lifetime to pay her back. I would also like to express my appreciation for Tony Adamucci, my knight in shining armor, who came to my rescue in a dark time, and for Peg Adamucci, an early reader, sounding board, and lifelong model of how it's done!

Thank you to Rosemarie Notoris—my m.i.w.—for telling me to take this road, and for loving me, always; to Bill Adamucci, for support in an awful hour; to Lisa

Zeiderman, my Amazon warrior, who fought for me, stuck by me, and forced me to grow up; to Pat Kennedy and Chris Johannet, for keeping me (relatively) sane; to Elena Lister, for being a true friend; to Jane Furse, for validation—now it's your turn; to Terry Iacuzzo, who promised me I could, and then told me to get to work; to Ron Burns, for providing me with my own personal writer's colony on the Upper West Side; and to Hugh Van Dusen, for lighting the path.

My utmost admiration and appreciation go to my extraordinary agent, Sharon Bowers, living proof that being a great businesswoman and a wonderful human being are not mutually exclusive. From her initial response to the manuscript (understanding such as I'd only dreamed of) to her Herculean persistence in finding the right publisher for it, working with her has been an unmitigated pleasure. Thanks, too, to Chelsey Emmelhainz, who originally acquired and championed the book at Arcade, and to the impressive team there, especially Cal Barksdale, a true editor's editor; copy editor Katherine Kiger, for her sharp eye and wonderful ear; production editor Jen Houle; and cover designer Erin Seaward-Hiatt.

Finally, my deepest gratitude goes to my son, Andrew—who makes life a joy.